Trouping Through Texas:

Clifford Ashby
and
Suzanne DePauw May

Harley Sadler and his Tent Show

Bowling Green University Popular Press
Bowling Green, Ohio 43403

CONTENTS

Harley as a cowboy Toby, with peaked eyebrows, huge freckles, and a blacked-out tooth. The boots had a soft counter, allowing him to "walk up" into the leg section. Photo taken in Shawnee, Oklahoma, 1917 or '18.

Introduction and Acknowledgments

HARLEY SADLER'S entertainment career began at about the time tent shows were reaching their peak of popularity, and concluded when air-conditioned movies, drive-in theatres and new styles of spectacle and sophistication drove the "rag opries" from the dusty vacant lots of American villages.

The tent show represents a brief but important phase of American theatre. In 1927, Don Carle Gillette, editor of *Billboard*, wrote a lengthy article on the subject for the *New York Times* in which he offered statistical evidence that the tented drama constituted "a more extensive business than Broadway and all the rest of the legitimate theatre industry put together."

According to records kept by *The Billboard*, there are at present 400 tent-theatre organizations scattered around the United States. Nearly all of them play a season of forty weeks or more—many run nearly fifty, and some never lay off at all. The shows, for the most part, have a repertoire of six to a dozen bills, and it is the usual policy to remain a week at each stand. Consequently, at a conservative estimate, 16,000 communities are served with theatrical performances each year through the medium of the tent show.

The legitimate drama, on the other hand, now has less than 500 houses in the entire country. About fifty of these are in five cities... while about fifteen other cities each have from two to five legitimate playhouses, so that the actual number of cities now getting Broadway stage attractions is around 300. The tent-drama, therefore, visits fifty-three places to every one visited by the Broadway drama.

Further comparison offered by Gillette show that the legitimate theatres presented a total of 80,000 performances compared to the tent show's total of 96,000. He estimated that the total attendance for legitimate productions throughout the country totalled 48,000,000 yearly, compared with a tent show total of 76,000,000. He added,

If the number of patrons attending the dramatic performances given by the Chautauqua units were added to the figure already given for the tent-shows the total would be equal to more than twice the number of playgoers that the legitimate theatre now serves.

For over four decades, tent theatres brought

1

entertainment to rural America. These troupes sold their wares in the marketplace, surviving (and often prospering) on their ability to make a profit from the box office—unlike the one-week-a-year Chautauqua, which was heavily subsidized by local merchants for the dual purpose of bringing culture and business to the community.

Rising from the ashes of thousands of local stock companies that had been destroyed, around 1900, by the monopolistic practices of the Theatrical Syndicate, tent repertoire, "repper-tore" as it was usually pronounced, filled the need for regional drama. While the Syndicate was searching for products that would merchandise equally well in the Maine woods, Georgia villages, and Texas oil fields, the tent companies were writing, adapting and performing plays suited to their own limited touring areas. Big city comedies about sex and high society were both foreign and offensive to these rural audiences; tent-reppers were careful to provide shows which related to the hopes, desires, moral values, problems and especially the humor of their patrons. Thus Toby, the most popular comic figure of tent rep, was portrayed as a farmer in the Midwest, a lumberjack in Oregon and Washington, a Swede in Minnesota, and a cowboy in the Southwest.

Harley Sadler was more than an entertainer. To call him a genuine folk hero would be to risk understatement: for many, he was as near a certifiable saint as ever emerged from the Baptist Church. He was almost universally adored, a best friend to senators, movie stars, mayors, grocery clerks, and the poorest, raggediest cotton chopper on the Texas High Plains. He was "old Harley" to an amazing cross-section of the population, most of whom he could call by name even though he saw them only one week of the year. To the young people who dreamed of "joining up" with a tent show and visiting far-off lands, "Mr. Sadler" was a name spoken with reverence, even a little awe.

In an era when anyone connected with theatre (*the-A Y-ter* in Texanese) was automatically assumed to be three steps down the road to perdition, Sadler carried about him an aura of respectability that silenced any criticism. Preachers who regularly inveighed against "the sinful delights of that gorgeous playing place, the theatre," were regular patrons at Harley's show, and would frequently move Wednesday night services to an earlier hour so that both religion and entertainment could be accommodated in the same evening. Failure of the minister to attend (and there were some who did not) left him somewhat isolated from his flock, unable to join the discussion of "what them actors done" in the weeks after the troupe had left town.

The Texas actor-manager's reputation has not diminished in the years since his passing. In 1976, almost thirty years after the last Sadler show had folded its tent, a revival by Texas Tech University brought out crowds of old friends and admirers eager to see the "New " Harley Sadler Show, yearning to recapture what remained one of their fondest memories of growing-up in Texas. This same year, an aging "cousin" who had originally gained election to Texas' politically powerful Railroad Commission on the strength of Harley's endorsement and a supposed kinship, almost rode the showman's ghostly coattails into the same office once again.

Harley, although a modest man by show business standards, could not help but be aware of his standing with the public, and late in life began looking for someone to write his life story. To help in this task, he assembled a roomful of memorabilia from his career: financial records, route books, correspondence, newspaper clippings, photographs, posters, advertising heralds, scrapbooks. A close friend of the showman's, an author of no small reputation, was invited to his Sweetwater home to discuss the possibilities of a book. The prospective biographer, a practicing newspaperman more accustomed to daily headlines than months of painstaking research, viewed the records with dismay. They were, he concluded, depressingly complete, would require countless weeks of reading, organizing, verifying, assimilating. Regretfully, he decided that he lacked the time the task would require.

Unfortunately, these records no longer exist. Shortly after Harley's death in 1954, his despondent widow turned these reminders of happier days into a memorial funeral pyre. Since that time, several biographies have been begun, but none has been completed. This study began as a master's thesis at Texas Tech University by Suzanne DePauw Ricker (May), who assisted in the research for this book. The present writing is by Clifford Ashby.

Four years of research and writing have gone into this task. Wherever possible, sources have been given for specific quotes, but documentation has proven a thorny problem. Any attempt at specific attribution for all the myriad sources would have buried each page in a deluge of footnotes, elaborations, and equivocations. Wherever possible, details and events have been checked for accuracy, but often the inclusion or rejection of a specific incident came down to a matter of a "feel" for the material. The manuscript has been read by many people familiar with the events as they happened, serving as a further check on accuracy. Perhaps the words of John Genest, who assembled in 1832 *Some Account of the English Stage* may be borrowed by way of apologia: "If anything be overlooked, or not accurately inserted, let no one find fault, but take into consideration that this history is compiled from all quarters."

Much of the material on tent shows and their operations was supplied by former troupers, many of them members of the Sadler company at one time. One of the greatest pleasures in writing this book has been that of making friends with what is surely the most delightful group of sex-, sept-, and octogenarians in existence. Active, interested and interesting, mentally and physically active, they are blessed with amazing powers of recall. The following troupers may take well-deserved bows for their share in retelling the Sadler story: Douglas Ackley, Harry Akin, Olive Grandi Berry, Henry and Mercedes Brunk, Ollie Brunk, Olan Burrows, Bart Couch, Jay Bee Flesner, Erman and Goldie Gray, Elizabeth Greaves, Rolland and Peggy Haverstock, Harve and Euna Holland, Nelson "Johnny" Kelley, Sue Kelley, Tommye Leavell, Gil Lamb, Robert LaThey Johnson, Trixie Mascue, Jere Mickel, Ethel Snow Myers, Joe and Marian McKennon, Kelly Masters, June Mundee, Harry and Dell Phelps, Al and Lynn Pitcaithley, Harold Rosier, Caroline Schaffner, Clarence Segrist, Bob Siler, Louise Hefner Sorensen, Lyle Talbot, and Paul and Daisy Thardo-Kalmbacher. Bows are also due the following youngsters whose canvas careers began in the 'forties: George Babb, James V. and Juanita Davis, Susan Babb Ewalt, Bill Gray, Flo Darling, and Kelly Masters, Jr.

Ferd and Gladys Sadler are certainly entitled to be listed with the troupers, but they were of greatest help in supplying details of Harley's personal life. Others who aided in this were: Norman Bonds, W.S. Chennault, Dr. I.F. Hudson, Mrs. Grady Hamner, Bob Huff, Phil Isley, Raymond W. Matthews, Marie Sadler McNeill, Dick Morehead, Joe Pickle, Linna Sadler Taylor, Mrs. J.H. Tubb, and Jean Wright.

Information on oil and assorted business activities was received from Maurice Brooks, J.E. (Ed) Connally, Tom

Gordon, Roy Paine, and John Womble. From the political scene, help came from Ralph W. Yarborough, former U.S. Senator; Allan Shivers and Preston Smith, former Governors of Texas; Ben Ramsey, former Lieutenant Governor of Texas and Chairman of the Railroad Commission; former U.S. Representatives Omar Burleson and George Mahon; former State Senator Pat Bullock; and former State Representative Sterling Williams.

Nancy Fortner Prentiss was responsible for rallying round the many friends of Gloria, the Sadlers' only child. Help came from Harriet Reaght Bishkin, Marjorie Stevenson Hager, Mickey Tubb Rea, Mary Paxton Roberts, and Dr. Charles Rosebrough.

Further aid, help, advice, correspondence and/or encouragement was supplied by the following: Les Adams, Katherine Boehrer, Dub Bolus, Winnie Lou Bounds, L.K. Boutin, Mary Broaddus, Diane Bunting, Mrs. M. Carlin, Nancy Carr, Mrs. Gerald Coston, Dr. Frank Counselman, W.B. Cox, Vera Culwell, Mary Dement, Mrs. Ralph Dorsett, George Eels, Tom K. Eplen, Rex Felker, Janice and Minnie Fewell., Mrs. Osborne Fisher, Alice French, Mrs. Beth Gill, Ruth Goddard, J. Evetts Haley, Dr. H. Clay Harshbarger, Odell Hogan, Edith Hopkins, Ocie Hunt, Mont Hurst, Jane Jenkins, Helen DeVitt Jones, Emma Joyner, Lou Keay, John H. Kitchens, Virginia Loop, T.C. Lusk, Mint Marshall, Dr. Jerry L. Martin, Nina Peebles, Mrs. Kenneth Penrod, Dr. A. Redwine, Mr. & Mrs. Jack Rennels, Mrs. J.C. Richardson, W.W. Rogers, Elenora Robison, Laura Sheridan, Mrs. Earl Shirley, Bryon Smith, Matt Sullivan, C.K. Teaff, Robert J. Tiffany, Mrs. Verlin Towle, Winifred Vigness, Mrs. Lee Walker, Frank J. Wallace, Ted Weaver, Dr. Holmes Webb, Prof. William Whittington, Mrs. Carmen White, Francis Mixson White and Mrs. V.A. Wright.

The following libraries and museums have aided in research: Texas Tech University Library and Ray Janeway, Cliff Hicks, Gloria Lyerla, Dot Myrick, and Frank Temple; the Southwest Collection of Texas Tech University and Sylvan Dunn, Beth Gill, David Murrah, and Tommy Whiteley; the Hertzberg Circus Collection of San Antonio and Betty King; the Austin-Travis County Library and W.D. Cooper; the Sweetwater Library and Bess Atkinson; the Sweetwater County Museum and Alithea Dunn; the Cameron Public Library and Louise Jamison; the Abilene Public Library and Jane Wissler; the *Abilene Reporter-News* Library and Constance A. Chapman; The National Society for the Preservation of Tent, Folk and Repertoire Theatre and James V. Davis, Joe Mauck, Caroline Schaffner, and Helen Virden.

The history of popular entertainment is just beginning to peep over the academic horizon. In 1977, the American Society for Theatre Research and the Theatre Library Association combined to host a conference on "The History of Popular Entertainment." Billed as "the first meeting of its kind," the results of the conference have been published in the following volume:

American Popular Entertainment: Papers and Proceedings of the Conference on the History of American Popular Entertainment. Edited by Myron Matlaw. Westport, Connecticut, 1979.

Described in the publisher's notice as "a seminal contribution to this new scholarly awareness of these aspects of popular culture," the collection includes "Trouping Through Texas: Harley Sadler and His Own Show," by Clifford Ashby.

Aside from this volume, remarkably little attention has been paid the tent show by publishers or scholars. The following list of books may be of interest to readers wishing to learn more about this overlooked aspect of American theatre:

McKennon, Marian. *Tent Show.* New York 1964

An account of the post World War II adventures of the Marian McKennon Players, under the management of Joe McKennon. The last tours were undertaken in partnership with Harley Sadler.

Mickel, Jere. *Footlights on the Prairie.* St. Cloud, Minnesota, 1974.

A history of the tent shows, with emphasis upon those touring the Midwest. Filled with details of life under canvas.

Schaffner, Neil, with Johnson, Vance. *The Fabulous Toby and Me.* Englewood Cliffs, New Jersey, 1968.

An as-told-to autobiography by one of America's best-known Toby comedians.

Slout, William. *Theatre in a Tent.* Bowling Green, Ohio, 1972.

A dissertation-based account of the origins and

development of the tent show. Professor Slout grew up under the canvas of his family's Midwestern show.

Wilmeth, Don B. *American and English Popular Entertainment.* Detroit, 1980.
An extensive bibliography covering many popular forms, but with very little material on the tent show. Lists a few dissertations and magazine articles in addition to the books already cited.

Spiritual and material encouragement has come from the following administrators of Texas Tech University. Without their aid, the research and writing of this book would not have been possible, nor could the New Harley Sadler Tent Show, an invaluable aspect of this historic reconstruction, have been presented. Thanks are due to Graves Blanton, Dr. Dilford Carter, Dr. Robert Ewalt, Dean Lawrence Graves, Dr. Clyde Kelsey, and Dr. Richard Weaver.

In the course of research, materials have been collected for preservation at Texas Tech's Museum, Library, and the Southwest Collection. Included are costumes, posters, scrapbooks, playscripts, photographs, and many hours of interviews recorded with people who were a part of the Sadler story. Sadly, more than a half-dozen of these interviewees have already passed from the scene, but at least a portion of their story has been kept from oblivion.

The manuscript of this book has been read, entire or in part, by the following people, who offered suggestions for improvement: Ruth Adams, Jonathan Ashby, Brooks Barr, Fred and Marge Beasley, Henry and Mercedes Brunk, Carol Chipman, Erman Gray, Marjorie Stevenson Hager, Bob Huff, Joe and Marian McKennon, Roy Paine, Al Pitcaithley, Tobyn Probasco, Nancy Fortner Prentiss, Mickey Tubb Rea, Mary Paxton Roberts, Dr. Charles Rosebrough, Gladys Sadler, Dr. William Slout, Linna Sadler Taylor, and Dr. Richard Weaver.

A special acknowledgement must be accorded Sylvia Ashby, a willing co-worker who has plowed her way through innumerable drafts of this manuscript. With admirable patience she has participated in countless dialogues relating to problems of research and composition; with equal patience she has listened to endless monologues on the same subjects. Her perceptive criticism, her clear insights, and her ability to ask pertinent questions, have proven invaluable.

Special recognition should also be given to Mary DePauw, who planted the seed which ultimately resulted in this book.

Texans are reluctant to speak ill of the dead, and in remembering such a well-loved figure as Harley Sadler, they are inclined to conceal even very minor faults from possibly unsympathetic probing. Presented in the following pages are the combined recollections of a great many people, not one of whom could be shaken in his belief that Harley represented the personification of the homely virtues. If there existed a hidden, secretly-sinning figure somewhere behind the public image, no amount of probing, questioning, doubting, or playing the devil's advocate has been able to uncover it.

What follows is the Harley Sadler that people remember. If the passage of time has smoothed out a defect or two and polished an occasional blemish, so be it. After all, what are folk heroes for, if not to glorify a little?

Chapter One

A Texas Boyhood: Stage-Struck in Stamford

HARLEY SADLER was a second generation American. His grandfather, Sterling C. Sadler, born in 1823, had emigrated from his native England, arriving in Jamestown, Virginia, around the middle of the nineteenth century. Sadler was originally an occupation name, but neither Sterling nor any of the three brothers who accompanied him to the New World were engaged in the making of saddles. Somewhat better read than most migrants, he married Louisa Jane, a native American of above-average education, and the two became Virginia schoolteachers.

Junius E., who was to become Harley's father, was born in 1858. At a fairly young age, he married Lula T., a girl of sixteen, and tried to settle down to a life of farming. Like many young men, he was restless; he dreamed of the limitless opportunities which could be found in the less settled regions of this still-new nation. Bundling up his wife and their few worldly possessions, he joined the westward migration of the many Americans who sought the promised land which always lay beyond the next hill.

By 1892, Junius had progressed as far west as the Ozark Mountains of Arkansas, where he worked a farm near the village of Pleasant Plains. His wife had already borne him three healthy sons, Luther, Edgar and Leonard, when, on September 4th, another male child made his squalling appearance. He was christened Harley Herman.

Even with four children, J.E., as Junius was called, was not ready to settle down to a life of bare subsistence. Like many farmers of the time, he lived with chronic dissatisfaction. A large, thickset man whose shoulders were stooped from years of bending over a plow, he was not at all reluctant to move his family to any place that might offer a better living. He bought a piece of land here, rented one there, sharecropped another, considered the homesteading possibilities a little farther west. A farmer could scratch out a living almost anywhere, but J.E. dreamed of the bumper money-crop, the acres of cotton, peanuts, corn, wheat, that would bring in hard cash. He wanted to provide his wife and children with those luxuries they knew about only from reading the pages of the mail order catalogue. In 1893, when Harley was a year old, the Sadlers left Arkansas for McClennon County, Texas. Hopefully, a farm near Waco could provide sweeter soil, gentler climate, and an escape from the malarial chills of the Ozarks. One crop proved different from those grown on the preceding farms: Fanny, the Sadlers' only daughter, was born here.

Around 1900, the lure of better land over the horizon put the family back on the trail. Loading goods and chattels, putting chickens in homemade crates, and tying the milk cow behind the wagon, J.E. moved his family once again, this time to a "better" farm in Hopkins County. The new location was over a hundred miles to the northeast, but the address was still Texas. Fernando (Ferd) Sadler, the last of six children, was born here, near the village of Cumby. All of them were healthy enough to survive infancy and grow into adulthood, no mean accomplishment in those days.

Like most farm families, the Sadler clan was largely self-sufficient, needing very little from the world outside. An acre or two of wheat was planted each fall, to be ground into flour at a nearby mill when it ripened in early summer. A plot of sugar cane supplied sorghum to satisfy the sweet tooth of the children. A vegetable garden near the house furnished fresh produce for the summer. For the winter months, beans and sweet potatoes were stored in cellars. (Irish potatoes were still something of a rarity on the frontier.) Peaches that could not be eaten were either made into peach butter or were halved, pitted and left to dry on the roof in the bright summer sun. The family cow provided milk for the children, and buttery cream so thick that it had to be spooned from the pitcher.

Beef and pork were smoked or salted if necessary, but most farm families organized primitive cooperatives, a half-dozen families butchering on consecutive weeks and sharing the fresh meat among themselves. The streams were full of plump yellow catfish, and the land provided turkey, quail, squirrel, rabbit, ducks and geese for the hunter. There were deer, too, although the increased cultivation was cutting into their population. All kinds of wild berries, plums and pecans could be had for the picking. Life was not particularly easy, requiring the combined efforts of the entire family to provide necessities and a few comforts; but it was not an unpleasant existence.

Dallas was only fifty miles from the Sadler farm, but no one thought of going there. A trip to town meant going to Cumby, a crossroads community consisting of a few houses, a general store, blacksmith shop, a sprinkling of churches, post office, and a restaurant which doubled as an early-day community center. Horse and mule-drawn freight wagons rumbled down the dirt streets, hurrying to meet the one daily train which arrived around noon on the East Line of the Red River Railroad.

Like most country families, the Sadlers made a Saturday afternoon trip to town to lay in a few supplies for the coming week, and to visit with friends and neighbors. Daily chores behind them, the afternoon was reserved for socializing, and the sidewalks would be filled with farmers standing by the lampposts. Clad in clean overalls and their next-to-best Sunday shirt, they leisurely discussed crops, cattle, the market, politics and the state of the nation. There was usually a stop at the post office which brought a letter from the family back East. The perennial domino game in the post office lobby disseminated more news than the weekly county newspaper.

Major events in the town of Cumby were Fourth of July celebrations, picnics, revivals, Democratic (but never Republican) rallies, fires, floods, and touring shows. The last mentioned was limited by the size of the town to little more than small medicine shows and carnivals, but these were always well attended. For the country child living in nineteen hundred, a ride on a wooden merry-go-round horse (propelled by genuine horsepower) was an exciting event, not a pale imitation of his daily rides on the farm animals.

The young Harley rejoiced when time came for these weekly visits to town. The lonely, isolated life of the farm was not for him; he needed people. As a small child he would watch wistfully as his father and brothers prepared for a day's work in the fields, and then ask, "Leonard looks kind of peaked, don't he?" This next-oldest brother suffered from occasional attacks of malarial fever, and each morning Harley hoped that Leonard would be left at the house so that he would have someone to play with. "Leonard looks kind of peaked," was spoken so often that it became a family byword.

When he was finally old enough to be taken to the fields with his brothers, Harley found that, even with companionship, he was not destined to be a farmer. Set to chopping countless weeds from unending rows of corn and cotton, he would keep his eyes on the horizon, hoping that the crown of a thunderhead would make its appearance. When one finally arrived on the edge of the cloudless sky, Harley would discourse darkly on the perils of thunderstorms. Finally, he would straighten up, take off his straw hat, and wipe the sweat from his face with a bright red bandanna. "Looks like it's coming this way," he would announce. Then, shouldering his hoe and looking at the stooped backs of the Sadler men, he would say, "Y'all can stay here and git struck by lightning if you want to—but I'm heading for the house." As he stalked down the crop rows toward the supposed safety of the tiny board-and-batten building that was home, his brothers smiled indulgently at each other as they watched the tiny retreating figure. Harley's penchant for avoiding stoop labor formed the basis for another family joke.

J.E. may have been a little like this middle son. By 1905, he had had his fill of farming. Packing up his family and belongings once again, he moved two hundred miles due west to Stamford, a small community where he could open a general store. Harley must have been overjoyed at the change; for as the son of the owner of the one store in the area, he was situated at the very hub of a little universe. Of necessity, everyone came into the Sadler store. There were also the social activities of the town to help fill his need for companionship: picnics, "speakings," supper-on-the-ground with visiting preachers, and ice cream socials for the young. Every August, families from the region assembled at nearby Spring Creek for a camp meeting. By early fall, there was little to do on the farms: crops were "laid-by" until they ripened for harvest. Ten days of sermons, singing, and socializing were moved outside the summer-hot church to a "brush arbor" built nearby. Families arrived in covered wagons (the first car was seen in Stamford in 1905). As each group came into camp, teams of men worked to unbolt the wagon box from the axles; then lifted box, canvas cover, and all from the frame and placed it on the ground, to serve as a floored tent until the family departed for home on the second Sunday evening of the meeting.

From all evidence, the Sadlers constituted a closeknit, affectionate family. J.E. was a loving if somewhat stern father, tending to be quick-tempered. "Raise up a child in the way he should go," he often said; and he kept a razor strop handy to be certain that "the way" was clearly delineated.

Ferd, the baby of the family, recalled that, "If I got a little out of line, said something smart at the table, Dad'd correct me, and maybe I'd answer smart again; then he'd say, 'Young man, one more remark and I'll get the razor strop.' And I knew he meant it!"

J.E.'s temper never came out in shouting and profanity; he saw no necessity for raising his voice. Although basically a religious man, he followed Abraham Lincoln's example in refusing to join a denomination. When anyone asked him what church he was a member of, he would reply, "No earthly organization." With the rest of the community, the senior Sadler attended Baptist, Methodist and Presbyterian churches on alternating Sundays, depending upon which one had the circuit-riding preacher in town for that week.

Lula, the mother, was softer, more openly loving than her husband, slower to anger. She could always remember some act of kindness that a person had done when someone spoke ill of him. Harley, in temperament, more nearly resembled his mother—although in later life he was not immune to the flashes of temper that characterized his father.

By the Stamford days, Sterling Sadler, the English grandfather and his wife, Jane, had come from Virginia to live with the family. Grandma was a long-suffering semi-invalid who used her poor health to keep her daughter-in-law in a state of bondage. Mother Lula could never plan on going to church services because Grandma Jane could be counted on to "take a turn" on Sunday morning. Uncomplainingly, this mother of six active children took on the added burden of caring for her husband's parents. But perhaps the evening hymn singing by the whole family—Fanny at the piano, Luther singing bass, and Myrtle, Edgar's young wife supplying a clear soprano—helped to compensate for the absence of regular church-going.

After his voice changed, Harley learned to sing bass, perhaps in imitation of his admired eldest brother, who had taken a turn at preaching but then settled upon a career as a businessman. Harley, however, was not scholarly and inward like Luther, who loved nothing better than curling up with a book among the feed sacks at the back of his father's store. Harley could not be classified as a "wild" boy, but together with Fanny, his young sister, he received perhaps a little more than his share of admonishment. Parents and teachers worked together in the matter of discipline, and the Sadler children usually received double punishment for a

The Sadler family around 1900.
Harley is on the left.

single transgression: Harley and his mischievous sister faced—or rather, about-faced—more than one encounter with a broad wooden paddle in the school's tiny cloakroom only to have their performance encored that evening by J.E.'s razor strop.

Through high school—from which he never graduated—Harley was a likeable but not exceptional boy. He played leading roles in the junior and senior class plays, and once nearly ended a performance by unexpectedly smearing catsup on his shirt as he fell from a make-believe gunshot. Occasional touring companies visited the Stamford Opera House, and the young actor liked to hang around backstage listening to the professionals tell of their adventures. When Joe Ward organized a town band in 1909, the seventeen-year-old Sadler was recruited as a trombone player. He learned to play several instruments, skills which enabled him to "double in brass" when he finally went on the road.

Life was not all play and diversion. Harley did his chores like the rest of the family. He delivered groceries for his father after school, driving a little wagon hitched to a pair of temperamental Spanish mules. A friend remembers seeing the skittish mules take off down Main Street one day, strewing delivery boy and bushel baskets full of groceries behind them. A concerned crowd gathered around the young boy who sat doubled up on the curbstone. He was bent over with laughter, not with pain: the joke was on him, but he could still enjoy it.

Fully grown, Harley stood about five foot six inches. He was small-boned, with a fair complexion and yellow-blond hair. His lopsided grin and slightly pointed ears gave him a pixyish expression, as if he were always smiling at some private joke. His features were so fine that on one of his early returns from the road, his cousin, Bessie Taylor, dressed him in one of her frocks and passed him off to friends as a visiting girlfriend.

Harley seemed, however, to possess the then-normal boyhood aspirations and ambitions, including the urge to become a professional baseball player. This was an era when almost every level bit of pasture was scarred by a well-trod diamond, when the sides of many a barn bore massive bruises showing where a would-be pitcher had spent lonely hours chunking a ball at a large knothole. Harley shared the almost-universal ambition to make the major leagues. In truth, he was not very talented, either at bat or in the field, but this did not lessen his desire.

He was possessed by another, even stronger, ambition, one which he kept to himself. "I have had," he once confessed to a reporter, "from my earliest childhood an unexplainable desire to get into show business." In 1909, at the age of seventeen, the desire became too strong to resist: he ran away from home to join the Parker Brothers' Carnival, traveling out of Houston.

Needless to say, his family was shocked and horrified. Children from good homes did not leave school, friends and family to join anything as disreputable as a carnival, then as now at about the bottom of the show business ladder of respectability. Many boys talked about running away from home, joining the circus or hopping a freight, but few actually did. The handful who left seldom got beyond the next county before homesickness or a visit from a grim-faced father—often accompanied by the local sheriff—convinced them that home possessed virtues as well as drawbacks.

The young Sadler not only left, but he stayed with the carnival for several months, despite disappointments. He had been lured away from home by the promise of a job as trombonist with a prospective carnival band. The musical ensemble never assembled, and Harley found himself working as a "spieler" on the midway, selling popcorn and cotton candy, doing whatever he could do to make a living. Anyone less in love with show business would have been cured of his affliction by this one experience.

Even though the teen-age runaway realized that carnival life was not for him, it did not lessen his appetite for a place in the entertainment world. Returning to Stamford late that fall, he quickly organized a vaudeville troupe, taking two friends, Carey Shell and Roy McGaines, into the company. The three made up in enthusiasm what they lacked in experience. "We were," Harley laughingly told a reporter,

without experience but we had plenty of nerve and we barnstormed our way to Kansas City. Our show, which consisted of seven acts of vaudeville and included medicine show sketches, was a financial success but physically dangerous. Our audience usually left before we completed the seven acts.

The Stamford trio broke up in Kansas City, and the best show-business job that Harley could find was as a billposter/advance man with the McDonald Company. Billposting was a minor industry at the time, requiring a large work force. These "knights of the brush" regarded themselves as skilled craftsmen and had formed their own union. Crews traveled a week ahead of the shows, putting up their gaudy advertisements. Moving about with a large boiler filled with glutinous paste, they fitted together a series of sheets into a large poster, taking care that there were no paste lumps or air bubbles, matching each seam as carefully as if it were wall paper in a living room. No smooth surface was exempt from their brushes: barns, buildings, billboards bearing other advertisements, telephone poles and trees—everything pastable bore polychrome evidence that a billposting crew had passed that way. These bills were a feature of the countryside, remaining until another crew pasted over them, or until wind, sun and rain reduced them to tattered fragments, barely discernible over the *CHEW RED MAN* sign originally painted on the barn.

Harley preceded the McDonald Company to California and then through the Northwest, advertising one-night stands of *Girl of the Golden West,* the drama by David Belasco which Puccini later made into an opera. After several months on the road, the troupe worked its way back to Kansas City, closing the run where it had begun.

After briefly being employed by an advertising company in Kansas City, the young actor joined a musical comedy company. He left the show in 1910, suffering from stomach pains. A plaintive letter from Parsons, Kansas, to his family brought an immediate response. Luther, his brother, arrived at his bedside on the next available train. This eldest of the six children tended to Harley's immediate needs, then bundled him onto the train for the trip home. Arriving in Stamford, the nineteen-year-old prodigal was warmly greeted by his family, and, it may be assumed, soon sat down to a dinner of fatted calf.

During Harley's absence, the family had moved to Avoca, a few miles from Stamford. J.E. had a different general store, but otherwise things were very much the same. Harley remained at home through the spring and summer of 1911, convalescing from his illness, whatever it may have been. Most stomach pains at that time were routinely diagnosed as the dreaded "appendicitis," but these pains were probably the first onset of the nervous stomach which was to plague the performer for most of his life. At any rate, the illness faded beneath the liberal applications of tender loving care and the bowls of chicken broth supplied by his worried mother. Undoubtedly she shook her head, sighed, and muttered the age-old mother's lamentation, "That boy just hasn't been eating right!"

The family discussions centering around this errant young man are not difficult to imagine. Obviously anything further to do with show business was absolutely unthinkable; the parents and the older brothers shouldered the responsibility of talking some sense into this rebellious middle son who had turned out so unexpectedly different from the other children.

"Look at you! Three years wasted and all you got to show for your time is a trunkful of funny-lookin' clothes and a bellyache."

"Harley, don't you want to make something of yourself, be respected in the community?"

"Hanging around with all that riffraff—and the kind of women you're meeting; well, I can just imagine!"

"Boy, you weren't raised up to fritter your life away. Look at your brother Luther: he's going to go into the bank and make something of hisself."

"You're smart enough, but you need an education these days to get anywhere.... Ever think of being a lawyer? The Good Lord knows you could talk the ears off a brass monkey."

"You need to get educated."

"Be somebody."

"Education .... Education .... Education!"

A chastened Harley succumbed to the family's arguments. The wardrobe trunk was put away in an unused corner of the woodshed, and the former actor embarked upon the pursuit of knowledge. A local Presbyterian minister arranged a tuition scholarship (around $40 a year) to Reynolds Academy, in nearby Albany. Determined to begin a new life, Harley enrolled in a "preparatory" course, apparently one intended to make up the deficiencies of his high school education.

Reynolds Academy, in 1911, was housed in a two-storied, nine-room brick and stone building. Within this structure, education from primary grades through college was provided by a faculty largely conscripted from local residents. The Presbyterian minister of Albany took time from his congregation to serve as president of the Academy and to teach Bible classes. The editor of Albany's weekly newspaper was principal of the school. The town dentist taught courses in law, government and business administration. An Easterner who had come west for his health found himself drafted as a professor of foreign languages.

Situated near the buckle of Texas' Bible Belt, Albany boasted of the wholesome atmosphere of their community. A 1909 newspaper article promoting Reynolds Academy stated,

Shackleford County is a prohibition county where the law is rigidly enforced by competent officials, backed by a public sentiment overwhelmingly opposed to the slightest violation of law. Drunkenness, therefore, is not seen on the street and there are no haunts of vice to tempt the pupils to go astray.

When this reformed black sheep of the Sadler clan arrived in Albany, he found a newly erected dormitory there to receive him and keep him from any possible temptation. The few students (of both sexes) who lived away from home were housed in this building. Harley earned his room and board here by waiting tables and washing dishes.

During these years, the Academy possessed something of a military air, with students required to keep their rooms ready for daily inspection. Military style punishments were doled out to those who were found deficient. Dr. Ricker, the dentist-turned-teacher, had been appointed Captain of the Albany branch of the National Guard, and he recruited students for his chronically undermanned detachment. Harley recalled in a 1950 interview with Ruby McGill Dodge that:

As Albany was a very small town and couldn't meet the Company quota from its civilians, the headquarters for the guard were in a room in the Administration Building, which also housed the guns and equipment. Most of the student body belonged to Captain Ricker's company.... I may have been a corporal, but I believe that I was a private in the rear ranks. We didn't have daily drills, as I remember it, but we did have some semblance of military discipline in the school. I vividly remember some of our maneuvers in the spacious hills north and west of the Academy with its cactus, rocks and mesquite bushes. Here we got our experience in field warfare.... Captain Ricker had traveled a great deal and had a flair for show business. He spent much time discussing it with me, as well as his past experiences and places we both had visited.*

The temporarily reformed actor was able to survive the first year of "preparatory and business administration courses" with no apparent difficulty. The next fall he returned to school bearing a multivolume set of *Blackstone's*

*Quoted from *Reynolds Presbyterian Academy and College,* by Ruby McGill Dodge, Belton, Texas, 1960.

Commentaries, a gift from Luther, who wished to further his brother's legal ambitions. Tiring of the regimented life in the dormitory, he opened a "tailor shop" in partnership with Milburn S. Long, a fellow student. In truth, the establishment did little more than laundry and dry cleaning. According to one reporter, Harley "bought a smoothing iron and washtub, scrubbed dirty garments and ironed the wrinkles out of 'em." "We slept in the back room," Harley recounted, "and took our meals with Mrs. Adamson."

Milburn Long, later to become an associate justice of the Court of Civil Appeals, should have provided Harley with a splendid example to follow. "He was," an older Harley remembers, "so studious, so determined, and so deserving that his success is no surprise to me." The example, however, was lost upon the stage-struck youth. Within a month after returning to Albany, the many volumes of Blackstone became as monotonous and look-alike as the endless rows of cotton he had cultivated as a boy. He began hanging around the Albany Opera House, and when a touring company offered him a job, he sold his books, gave the cleaning business to his astonished partner, and left town.

After this engagement came to an end, Harley did a few weeks of small parts and walk-ons with the respected North Brothers Stock Company in Fort Worth. This was followed, he later told a newspaper interviewer, by a longer but less profitable engagement.

After that I went to Waco and got in with the Richard Mandell company which was playing the season there. It was my first time to play responsible parts and I played the rest of the season—without pay. I was afraid to ask for salary for fear I would get fired.

From the end of 1912, when he closed with Mandell, until Christmas of 1914, various sources provide the names of a series of companies and places, not all of which can be verified. Sadler definitely played twenty-six straight weeks in 1913 with Rentfrow's Jolly Pathfinders, in Texas City. At the time, this small town near Houston contained 25,000 National Guardsmen, called up to protect the southern border from possible onslaughts by Pancho Villa and his army of what were assumed to be *banditos.* Although there were a few border skirmishes and, of course, the celebrated invasion of Mexico by General Pershing and his army, the troops in Texas City languished hundreds of miles from the action. Not surprisingly, these citizen-soldiers, bored by

WONDERLAND FLOATING THEATRE

=PRESENTS=

The Call of the Woods

A Comedy Drama of the Canadian Woods
With Special Electrical and Scenic Effects

CAST OF CHARACTERS

Dave Ferguson, a lumber Jack........Norman F. Thom
Willis Hughes, Dave's half brother....... Jack Howard
Doctor Quackenbush, the village doctor...Howard Hack
Eben Quackenbush, the doctor's son.....Harley Sadler
Flapjack Lescant, a trapper...... .....Fletcher Averitt
Mrs. Hughes, the mother ....Miss Eva Morgan
Doris Keene, an heiress ....Viola Wills
Hilda Lescant, Flapjack's daughter........ Miss Bartine

SYNOPSIS OF PLAY

ACT FIRST—Home of Mrs. Hughes near Moose Jaw, Canada. Night. Early autumn. Mrs. Hughes discusses with Doris about her two sons, Willis being her favorite. Hilda expresses her love for Willis. Doctor, Eben and Flapjack visit the home of Mrs. Hughes. Dave also pays his mother a visit, and is later driven from her door, accused of stealing her money.

ACT SECOND—Exterior of Flapjack's cabin one week later. Evening. Flapjack thinks Hilda is in love with Dave, and does not approve of him. Willis agrees to help matters along. Eben seeks his "paw." Finds him and they mix. Willis lies about Dave to Doris. Dave pleads his love for Doris. Willis tries to elope with Hilda. Dave intercedes and drives Willis from the place.

ACT THIRD—Interior of Dave's lodging near the saw-mill. The day following. Eben visits Dave and so does the doctor. Willis chances in also and tries to induce Dave to leave the country. Hilda scorns Willis. Dave is accused of murder.

ACT FOURTH—Judge's chambers in court house three months later. The folks discuss the trial. Doctor proposes to Mrs. Hughes. Dave has no hopes of acquittal. Hilda arrives just in time. All is well that ends well.

A program from Harley's season on the showboat. Eben Quackenbush is a silly kid role, akin to the Toby part.

inactivity, sought entertainment. Rentfrow's, a large and respected company, played for six months to overflow houses.

In 1914, Harley became principal comedian with the Tarbett and White Stock Company, and moved from there to an engagement with the Billy House Stock Company, a tabloid company playing the Alamo Theatre, in Waco. (These "tab" shows were very popular at the time, featuring a chorus line, comedians, singers and variety acts.) During this period of growth he was probably (but not certainly) a performer with the Glide Stock Company, Fairfield's Stock Company, and Rucker's Comedians, the latter a tent-medicine show run by Dr. H.B. Rucker.

Cooley and Pell's Wonderland Floating Theatre, a showboat coursing the Mississippi and its tributaries, served as the young Sadler's home for one or two seasons. An undated program which can be placed somewhere in the early 'teens shows him playing the "silly kid" role in *Call of the Woods*, a comedy-drama about life in the Canadian wilderness. Harley himself recalled these showboat days as an idyllic interlude in the otherwise frenetic activity of tent show life. Much of the hard physical labor involved in touring was eliminated: there was no sweating, arduous put-up of tent, no tear-down after a few days of playing. The actor was spared the hurried, harried packing of wardrobe trunks, the endless moves in and out of a succession of hotels and rooming houses. The shift to a new location meant little more than a pleasant nap in a deck chair while a puffing little tugboat pushed the floating theatre from one river community to another.

The waterfront was usually in the rougher part of town, so there was little after-show socializing: actors were afraid to walk back to the boat late at night. In the afternoon, however, a member of the troupe might stroll downtown to bask in the admiration of the towers who hung goggle-eyed around the soda fountain as he ordered a double-egg malted, the most expensive item on the menu. For diversion, they swam alongside the boat in the sluggish Mississippi, or jug-fished for huge catfish which sometimes weighed over a hundred pounds.

During this time, perhaps when the Wonderland ended its season at Peoria, Illinois, Harley had his one and only brush with the world outside provincial theatre. With a friend he went to Chicago, determined to make it in the Big Time. The duo had put together a vaudeville act which included a monologue Harley had used successfully on the showboat. Their failure was total, and the two young men existed by passing out handbills for a Chicago department store. For a time, their diet consisted of soda crackers and nickel hunks of rat cheese.

By December 1914, the drifting, rootless, apprentice part of Harley's professional life had come to an end. He settled down to several years of performing in the more stable environment of Roy E. Fox's Popular Players, generally regarded as one of the finest, most successful tent repertoire companies in the nation. Their touring was limited to Texas, with headquarters in Sulphur Springs, not too far from Harley's home town.

By this time, the fledgling actor had amassed a wealth of experience. He had performed in showboat, vaudeville, tab, stock, medicine, tent, and one-night-stand situations. His advancement had been reasonably steady. He had moved up the provincial show-business ladder to a position as second comedian with a highly respected company. His salary was still ridiculously small, but at least he had the reasonable assurance that his new manager would meet the payroll each week. At the time he joined the Fox company, Harley had just reached the age of twenty-two.

Chapter Two

Learning the Ropes: Lessons from the Fox

MOST YOUNG ACTORS follow the checkered, erratic hand-to-mouth kind of existence that Sadler experienced. Sooner than most, however, he found steady employment with a reputable company. In 1915, he became second comedian with the Roy E. Fox Popular Players, called by *Billboard* "without doubt, one of the most thoroughly equipped tent shows traveling." Fox employed a company of forty, and presented his entertainments under a sixty-five by one hundred thirty-five foot tent which seated two thousand people. By 1920 he was successful enough to add "a beautiful drawing room Pullman, for use as his private car." He christened it "Hazel," for his second wife.

Fox was not born to the baronial splendor of a private parlor car; he achieved this status by being one of the best tent show operators in the country—and one of the shrewdest. "I'm a fox by name and nature," he used to boast, and anyone who ever discussed salary with the foxy manager could testify to the accuracy of that statement! Harley's income with the Fox troupe never exceeded fifteen dollars a week—even after he became the principal comedian with top billing.

A story demonstrating Fox's methods concerns an actor who complained to his boss about failure of the company to provide more than one egg for breakfast. With the actor in tow, Fox marched over the cook tent where he informed the startled chef that this actor was to have as many eggs as he wished! Ushering his grateful employee to the door, the manager turned around, caught the cook's eye, and emphatically held up *one* finger.

The owner/manager of the Popular Players was a self-made man, a rare combination of stage-struck youth and capable businessman. Born of Pennsylvania Dutch stock in 1879, in McKeesport, Pennsylvania, he began operating his own Punch and Judy show at the age of nine. By ten, the youthful entrepreneur had prospered enough to buy a team and wagon, enabling him to play a circuit of school playgrounds in the area. He made a substantial profit from the penny offerings of the enchanted children, most of whom were only a little younger than he.

At the age of sixteen, Fox joined the Harkness Family Show. Hired mainly to present his Punch and Judy, he also did a specialty act as a ventriloquist, and played "utility" roles in the dramatic presentations. Within a few years, he had married a Harkness daughter and shortly thereafter became a part-owner of the show. As burnt-cork comedy grew in popularity, the advertising reflected a change in format as well as ownership: "HARKNESS AND FOX MINSTRELS," proclaimed their posters.

Early in the century the company left the familiar Pennsylvania territory and began working slowly westward, playing through Missouri and Arkansas in 1906. When Fox's wife died, the Harkness stake in the management seems to have faded: as the company crossed the Red River into Texas, around 1910, the name changed to FOX'S LONE STAR MINSTRELS. Business was apparently good for the young owner and he kept his company in East Texas for several years, avoiding such metropolises as Houston, but doing good box office business at such crossroads communities as Groveton, Diboil, Onalaska, Tenaha, Carthage and Center. By 1912, when the countryside was almost buried in a proliferation of blackface comedy companies, the show changed to the ROY E. FOX POPULAR PLAYERS.

A listing of the company published by the *New York Clipper* in 1915 gives some insight into the kind of entertainment that was being presented. Top billing went to the principal comedian/stage director, Leon Bostwick, who had been with Fox for a number of years. The rest of the company consisted of

Sam Bright, juvenile leading man; Bones Wilkenson, characters; Harley Saddler, light comedy [his name was chronically misspelled]; Clare C. Copeland, Ed. Copeland, and Roy Farmer, general business; Dottie Sheffield, ingenues; Erin Bright, soubrettes; Nellie Thardo, grand dames; Minnie Wardell, characters; Audress Walsh, heavies; and Hazel Fox [Roy's pretty new wife], popular and versatile leading woman.

According to the *Clipper*, the actors provided a range of between-act entertainment:

The vaudeville with the show is in itself a feature, including: Dutch and

become a winning candidate. The owner/manager thanked the delegation for their consideration, but firmly declined to run. He had, he said, run his own operation far too long to ever be able to learn the arts of political compromise. Besides, wasn't he already, "The Governor"?

Fox was regarded as one of the leaders of the tent show industry, and the two national theatrical weeklies competed for his attention, knowing that many owners would follow his lead in placing their advertising. In 1915, Fox took a trip East while his company took Christmas vacations, visiting the offices of the established *Clipper*. Shortly thereafter the following extravagant and ungrammatical praise appeared in its pages:

Roy E. Fox is justly entitled the Monarch of Tented Theatricals.... The secret of Fox's success is his untiring efforts, his desire and determination to have only the best. His genial temperament and his humanitarianism. He is an ardent believer in fraternity, and permeates his daily life with its teaching. A good fellow, always willing to extend a helping hand and ever ready to contribute to charity. He is deservedly popular, and loved and respected by all who know him.

The Texas showman also visited the Cincinnati offices of *Billboard*, that upstart competitor of the established *Clipper*. He must have created a favorable impression, for the Fox likeness appeared on the cover of the New Year's issue, accompanied by a story which rivalled the other weekly in fulsome praise:

He stands for all that is best in the business. He is widely esteemed and highly thought of and universally honored by his confreres, and firmly entrenched in the affections and favor of the public.

He is a gentleman in every sense of the word.

Fox had an almost Barnum-like knack for getting into print at the slightest pretext. Not infrequently touring tent companies would vanish from the pages of *Billboard* for weeks at a time, usually because the company correspondent hadn't bothered to send in a report of their activities. Not so with Fox: he saw to it that his correspondent wrote complete reports—and every week! Whatever happened to the Popular Players was newsworthy. Articles covered The Governor's trip to his medicine factory in Sulphur Springs; Mrs. Fox's approaching motherhood; an order for new steel baggage cars; the purchase of a five-passenger automobile with a Knight motor, electric fans for the parlor car, and a complete menu for the company's Thanksgiving banquet.

There was little that did not provide grist for Fox's publicity mill. In 1915, the year of his trip East, the manager allowed the performers to vote themselves a three-week (unpaid) layoff at Christmas time. The *Billboard* correspondent for the company dutifully reported:

Magnanimously disregarding the big financial loss entailed in foregoing the always record Christmas and New Year's business, Manager Fox not only ungrudgingly but enthusiastically yielded to the wishes of his employees.

The following year, Fox's position on Christmas vacations had taken a hundred eighty degree turn, and he played Scrooge to the troupe's collective Bob Cratchit. This also provided publicity. Even the traditional Christmas layoff was cancelled, and the very popular players stayed on the boards in San Angelo throughout the holidays. Sadler, who happened to be serving a brief stint as *Billboard* correspondent, wrote cheerfully, "The company had a Christmas tree and many beautiful presents were received by different members. Christmas was all that could be desired." Undoubtedly there was some grumbling around the tree as actors found themselves unexpectedly absent from accustomed family gatherings. Harley noted in his next sentence, "Mr. Fox spent the holidays with his wife, who is visiting her mother in Albuquerque."

The Governor took what free publicity could be had, but he also believed in spending money for advertising. This was an era when most tent shows limited their ad expenses to the window cards and posters which brought in an immediate return at the box office. They placed ads in the trade newspapers only when they were hiring or looking for scripts, but Fox was concerned with product identification. Beginning in 1916, a two-column, one-inch announcement appeared weekly in the pages of *Billboard*, stating simply:

ROY E. FOX

Fifteen years without closing

per. address, Box 171, Sulphur Springs, Texas

These few words were framed on the sides by small oval pictures of Roy and his wife, Hazel.

While the young Sadler was never to acquire Fox's

technique for extracting from reporters the kind of boot-licking overpraise that was quoted earlier, there was still plenty for him to learn from his employer. Harley could not have found a better teacher to instruct him in such matters as promotion, advertising, and public relations.

Public relations, a term that had not yet been invented, came as easy as breathing to a man like Fox. A natural joiner who loved being a part of as many groups as possible, the genial manager was simultaneously a Knight of Pythias, an Odd Fellow, a 32nd degree Mason, a Shriner, a Knight Templar, a Moose, an honorary life member of the Elks—in addition to numerous show business clubs and organizations. He visited very few towns where there was not at least one group of men he could claim as brothers.

The company was expected to be as friendly and outgoing as their employer. Actors visited ranches, went on fishing expeditions, were taken bear hunting, attended suppers and picnics, routinely provided free entertainment for civic events. The company became a part of each community; under Fox's genial management, the traditional isolation of the strolling player all but vanished.

However, publicity and public relations were only part of the Fox formula for success: he was very careful to provide a very marketable product. Although his Popular Players were regarded as one of the best companies on the road, The Governor was, as *Billboard* observed, "constantly seeking methods of improvement." Writing of his own accomplishments in 1917, Fox recorded with Barnumesque enthusiasm that,

I have spent years in study of seating arrangements and stage equipment so that my patrons may be as comfortable and feel as secure as in their own home playhouse, while my performers can feel as much at home on my stage as if they were on the largest theater stage. I have spared neither time nor money in making each performance a complete scenic production. Instead of "tie-on" diamond dye stuff I find well painted flat scenery just as practical and much more effective. A properly lighted stage with all the necessary off stage strips, spots, and floods, is just as easily operated as a couple of half-filled borders. With my "A" frame stage rigging I am given height enough to properly dress any scene and at the same time remove all poles from the stage front, giving each seat a clear proscenium opening with no poles as obstructions. I find that a well lighted portable theater lobby is just as practical as the old marquee and much more attractive. I find it just as easy to heat a tent—if properly constructed heating plants are installed—as it is to heat a theater, and, in a great many cases, more so. I have established a record of seventeen years without closing. During the winter months I play where local conditions will warrant good business regardless of the weather, and have yet to hear a serious complaint from either patron or performer that the tent is not comfortably warm at all times....

I find the difference in the expense of carrying a good band and orchestra, at the expense of a mediocre one so small that it would be foolish to think of the saving. I try at all times to have absolutely the best band and orchestra in the repertoire game.

A full cast of capable dramatic artists and absolutely feature vaudeville are just as essential as the poles which hold up the top. I have never lied to or fooled my patrons, but try to give them exactly what I promise.

Fox was the first of the tent show managers to deal with the traffic problems presented by the increasing number of motor cars. He established pedestrian safety zones, provided parking lot attendants, and enforced a speed limit of ten miles per hour in the vicinity of the tent. His attention to such details served as a useful model upon which the young Sadler was to build when he became a manager.

Harley also learned about the perils of the weather while he was on the Fox show, but here Mother Nature was the tutor. Gale force winds were an expected part of a normal spring season in the Texas Panhandle, constituting little more than a passing annoyance to Fox's experienced canvasmen; they had weathered many storms with little more than minor rips and rents. In 1915, Sadler's first year with the show, Fox experienced what he was later to term his "only serious blowdown in seventeen years of continuous showing." The tent was struck by a full-fledged tornado one March evening as the company was playing in Post, a community nestled against the Caprock escarpment on the edge of the Texas High Plains. O.A. Peterson, a musician with the show, sent a lengthy account of the blowdown to the *Billboard.*

The disaster came without warning. One baby was instantly killed, and about thirty people were more or less seriously injured.

I have seen many blowdowns during my third of a century in the show business, but this was the most sudden and the most complete work of destruction I have ever witnessed....

At the approach of the storm Mr. Fox and Mr. Lighthall ["Doctor" Lighthall was the company's snake-oil specialist at the time], commenced distributing rain checks to the audience, and had supplied about half of those in the reserved seats when things began to happen. Mr. Fox ordered everybody to pass out as quickly as possible, but the audience was slow to move.

I grabbed my instrument and ran out on the windward side, and had gone about ten feet when the big electric light in front of the tent (one thousand candle power) exploded with a loud report. In another moment there was the sound of snapping ropes and pulling stakes, followed immediately by the crash of general breakage and the falling of poles and seats. The tent was ripped into shreds over the heads of the people and scattered over the surrounding plains.

The audience made a rush for the Double U ranch building, which was thrown open to them by the C.W. Post Company.* The wounded were carried in there and given first aid.

One of our working men, known as "Dutch," was injured internally by a falling pole, and is now in the hospital at Post, with slight chance for recovery.

Of our people, the most seriously injured is Leon Bostwick, our stage director and leading man. He could possibly have saved himself had he not stopped to pick up a little child which had in some manner become separated from its mother.

Harley Saddler (sic!) also found himself lying on the railroad track, slightly bruised, but not seriously hurt. He heard Bostwick groaning near him, and with the aid of our stage carpenter, assisted him over to the Santa Fe depot. While here they closed a gash in his head by tying his hair across it, which proved to be exactly the right thing to do, as the doctor at the hospital afterward told them. The doctor himself closed the wound in this manner after cleansing and sterilising it.

Sterling Williams, who was later to serve with Harley in the Texas Legislature, found himself in the audience that night. He recalls helping lay the injured on the map tables at Post Company headquarters. He also vividly remembers the appearance of the young Sadler as he walked into the room that night. The Toby freckles of his makeup were smeared into blood-red blobs, lip rouge stretched to one of his ears, and his forehead gleamed fish-belly white where a red wig had perched before the gale blew it away. A woman helping one of the doctors glanced up, then stared in horror at the actor. "Dear God!" she shrieked, "Somebody help that poor man over there. He's dying!"

According to Williams, houses were unroofed and trees uprooted by the force of the storm. Apparently Dutch, the canvasman, recovered from his injuries, but a small girl had been trampled to death in the stampede of the audience. Wind, however, is regarded as a condition of living in West Texas, and Fox was not held accountable for this catastrophe. The performers picked up what they could of their belongings while their manager made arrangements for a spare tent, stored in Stamford, to be sent to their next location. The tour continued after this major disaster with no more than the loss of a day or two. A few weeks later, after the shock had worn off, and the sorrow of the child's funeral—for which Fox bore the expense—had faded a little, the Popular Players returned to Post to redeem the rain

*C.W. Post, of Post Cereal fame, began selling land here in 1907, helping set off an early land boom in the Texas Panhandle.

checks that had been given out on that fatal night. Life on the frontier allowed little time for grieving.

Fox stayed late in the Panhandle the winter following the blowdown, not turning southward until the blue northers had blanketed the High Plains with hard-driven snow. His tent was equipped with double sidewalls, and with seven large stoves the company could, as Fox boasted, "play anywhere regardless of weather." In October, 1916, the troupe appeared for a short engagement in Amarillo's Grand Theatre, their first performances under a roof in over two years.

This same year, an eventful one for the young Sadler: Leon Bostwick, Fox's principal comedian, left to try his luck in the East, and Harley fell heir to his parts. He was now top banana, entitled to first billing on the company lists. As if to mark his entry into tent show stardom, *Billboard* carried a one column cut of Sadler, grinning lop-sidedly from the corner of the tent rep page. This time his name was spelled correctly.

Harley's abilities as a leader became quickly apparent. "Since the change in cast the players seem to be putting more energy and life into the parts. Each one on the show is trying to outdo himself or herself, and the company is improving every day," wrote Eddie Copeland, the *Billboard* correspondent. Business progressed from very good to superb, so much so that Copeland's glowing accounts took on a somewhat defensive air. In reporting an SRO opening in Midland, he felt it necessary to add:

In my letters I open with the same sentence so many times that no doubt many readers question my truthfulness. Anyone who has ever traveled with the Fox show through this territory knows that I speak the truth, for his business is an assured fact when he opens, the weather being the only thing to handicap him. The weather has been ideal for the past three weeks.

Fox, with his typical shrewdness, was able to use the excitement of World War I not only to demonstrate the patriotism of his company but also to fill his tent with enthusiastic spectators. Troop trains criss-crossed Texas, heading for training camps or to the Mexican border where, rumor had it, Pancho Villa was poised for a full-scale invasion. In Big Spring, when troop trains stopped every evening for an hour's rest on their way to Fort Bliss, they were met by large crowds of flag-waving citizens. Fox was there also, with his street band in full uniform. After

Roy E. Fox's Christmas ad in Billboard, *shortly after Harley became principal comedian, in 1916.*

cheering the trainloads of doughboys on their way, the excited crowd was in no mood to return home, and most followed the band back to the tent. The company enjoyed two weeks of overflow attendance in this tiny town.

Early in 1917, Harley had his first chance to appear as a principal comedian before a hometown audience. The Fox tent was pitched at Avoca, and everyone who traded at J.E.'s store came to see the Sadler boy, the one who ran away from home because he wanted to be an actor. By curtain time, the tent was crammed to overflowing with friends, relatives and well-wishers. That night, the audience clapped, cheered and whistled themselves into a near-frenzy. Harley, as he was later to tell the story, played with double his usual energy, and the rest of the cast, caught up by the feverish excitement of the occasion, tried to keep pace. It was nothing if not a full-blown theatrical triumph.

After the show, a very happy young performer greeted friends backstage. His mother and father, not quite used to being the parents of a celebrity, hung back in a corner. Their son, perspiring freely and still breathing heavily from the exertions of the evening, rushed over as soon as he spied them through the crowd surrounding him. J.E., grinning from ear to ear, pumped Harley's hand vigorously as he threw an affectionate arm around his shoulder—but Mother Sadler sat quietly on a wardrobe trunk, staring down at the floor.

"Well, Mamma," said Harley after an awkward silence, "What'd you think of the show?"

Mamma continued her study of the scarred wooden floor. "I guess as how it was pretty good," she said finally, tracing a crack in the boards with the toe of her high-button shoe. "But, Harley," she said, looking up into her son's happy face, "don't you think it's time you got a job?"

But if his mother didn't fully appreciate Harley's theatrical talents, there was another women who did. Shortly after his Avoca triumph, the young actor married a girl from Cameron who had been baptized Willie Louise Massengale, but who was known as Billie. As Harley and his wife were later to recount the tale, their marriage climaxed a whirlwind, three-day courtship and an out-the-bedroom-window elopement. According to Paul Thardo—Kalmbacher, events were not quite so dramatic, since the couple had met when the show played Cameron, a town in Central Texas, several months before the elopement, and a steady correspondence had ensued.

These facts seem fairly certain: Billie, who worked in the city clerk's office in Cameron, first met her future husband when he came to her desk to pay the license fee for the Fox show. That night, at the show, he contrived to slip her a note scribbled on a gum wrapper asking for a date. Billie accepted the invitation: like a great many girls, she had a crush on this winsome young actor.

The infatuation apparently ripened into true love. The next time the show came to town, Billie feigned a headache and sent her family to watch (unknowingly) the antics of their future son-in-law while she remained at home packing a suitcase. When the family returned, Billie was apparently asleep, but as soon as they had retired, she slipped out the door to a waiting automobile. With the young couple was Ed. Thardo (a period always marked the abbreviated name), almost a second father to Harley, who had come along to vouch for the fact that the bride was of legal age. Thardo also had to advance the young actor enough money to pay for the marriage license.

The next day, when the Massengale clan learned the cause of their daughter's absence, they were as upset as the Sadler family had been when Harley left home with the carnival. Her father, town marshal of Cameron, and her hulking elder brother arrived at the Fox tent determined to bring their girl to her home—and to her senses! They were met by the Senior Thardo, himself an imposing six-footer who played villains on the show when he was not doubling as a contortionist or throwing knives at his wife. "Mr. Ed." must have presented a persuasive argument: Billie remained with her new husband and the Massengale men went home empty-handed.

The edgy peace established by Thardo quickly dissolved into a love feast. No one could long dislike Harley Sadler, and he quickly became a member of the Massengale family—and the Massengales became a part of show business: Billie became a trouper, Mrs. Massengale, "Mamma Lou," toured many years with her son-in-law, and Billie's large, raw-boned brother, Burnie, quickly became devoted to his dimunitive brother-in-law, spending most of his adult life working for him on the road as a canvasman.

Everyone expected the young couple to settle down to wedded bliss as members of the Fox company. Many single actors married small town girls they had met on tour, and most of these girls, called "non-professionals" by *Billboard*, quickly adjusted to life with the strolling players. Billie was

A flapperish Billie Sadler, about the time of her marriage to Harley.

young, pretty and as likeable as her popular husband. Lacking any acting experience, she earned her keep by selling tickets, sacking popcorn, helping with medicine sales, keeping books for the company.

According to a *Billboard* story, marriage automatically granted Harley an exemption from the draft that was hanging over so many young men, but people who knew him at this time felt that his health may also have been a factor in his failure to serve in the Great War. Whatever the reason, this exemption seemed to guarantee a bright future with the Fox Players.

Business concerns involving his Sulphur Springs medicine factory combined with chronic malarial chills had kept Fox away from the show for most of 1917. Ed. Thardo managed the company in his absence, apparently with little difficulty. The nation was in the middle of a wartime prosperity, and money rolled in at the box office. In November, Fox ordered a mammoth tent, one which would seat three thousand spectators, together with "an up-to-date lighting system and all equipment connected with a first-class, modern tent theater."

Sadler was never to play under the new canvas. The *Billboard* correspondent for Fox reported with a certain surprise that their principal comedian was "closing with the show," leaving to join the Glen Brunk Company. Undoubtedly money was at least part of the reason for his leaving. Brunk was paying fifty dollars a week for a couple like the Sadlers, far more than The Governor could ever bring himself to part with. Moreover, the newlyweds were given the "banner concession," entitling them to fifty percent of the proceeds from the advertising signs which ringed the proscenium. (Billie, dressed in her most fetching attire, would sell these ads to the local merchants while Harley attended to the painting and lettering.)

Money, though, was only part of the reason for Harley's leaving the safe haven of the Fox Company. Brunk offered him not only the title of principal comedian but also that of stage director. The latter had always eluded him with the Popular Players. When Leon Bostwick quit the company, Harley had taken over the actor's leading roles, but Dutch Sheffield became the director. When Sheffield left, Joe Reed took over the director's assignment. Reed left to be with his dying father in the East, and C.C. Copeland fell heir to the title. Apparently, Copeland's appointment was the last straw; shortly after that event, Harley announced that he and his young bride were joining the Brunk organization.

Four Brunk brothers—Glen, Fred, Henry and Charley—together with an uncle, L.D. Brunk, maintained a position of leadership in the tent show industry. Originally musicians, they regarded themselves more as management experts than as performers, appearing onstage only as necessity dictated. At one time, the Brunks boasted of nine touring companies, although the actual total may have been somewhat less.

Eventually each brother had his own company and his own touring range. Glen played mainly through Kansas and Oklahoma, although he did sometimes venture into Texas and New Mexico. The Sadlers did very little touring with him that first season, since the tent was put away for the winter not long after they joined the company in September. After Brunk closed, the young couple appeared with Wil-Bucks Comedians, a small Oklahoma company playing the village opera house circuit.

The Buck of Wil-Bucks was J.A. Buckingham, who served as company manager while the Sadlers were with the show. The Wil- was Fred Wilson, regarded by many historians as the first man to crystalize the Toby role which was to become the mainstay of tent drama. However, Wilson was not with the company during the time Harley was playing the Toby parts for Wil-Bucks.

Billie probably had her first taste of acting with this little troupe: a company list includes a "Louis Sadler," among the women members. This seems likely to be a typo which should read "Louise," Billie's usually unused middle name. From this brief tour came the often reproduced picture of Harley as an early cowboy Toby, complete with woolly chaps, freckles, blacked-out teeth, and silly-kid grin.

By the spring of 1918, Harley and Billie were again working for Glen Brunk, touring the Barbour circuit of Oklahoma theatres. The indoor season closed in Ada, on March 26th, and less than a week later, the company opened under canvas in nearby Mangum. Harley was once again billed as comedian/director, while Billie received the title of "Business Manager." This was probably a polite term for ticket seller, since Glen always kept a close eye on the bookkeeping.

In July of 1918, with the war at its height, Brunk was drafted and sent to France, as a musician. With a great many admonitions and some misgivings, he turned the operation of his company over to his twenty-six-year old comedian. Glen may not have been much older than Harley, but he had been a successful manager for several years. Sadler had never run a company before.

Glen need not have worried, for the youthful Harley was able to inspire an almost fanatic loyalty in those about him. Actors and crews always worked hard and performed well for the Texan. Moreover, Harley had absorbed some show business wisdom in his years of knocking about: hearing that the Texas and Oklahoma crops had failed because of prolonged drought, he kept the show on the same lot in Wichita, Kansas, where Glen had left it. By changing the bill three times a week, he was able to do a very profitable business until cold weather forced him to close.

For the winter, Harley took Bob Graves, a Wichita musician, into partnership, and together they leased the Liberty Theatre, embarking upon a season of plays using most of the Brunk company of actors. The undertaking proved a disaster. They had no more than opened than a feather-bedding stagehand's union began adding unneeded and unwanted workers to the payroll, causing expenses to skyrocket. At the same time, the entire nation fell into the grip of the dread Spanish influenza, "swine flu" in today's parlance. The epidemic of 1918 reached the proportions of a national disaster. Theatres, schools, even churches were closed to prevent the spread of the disease, and almost everyone wore a litle bag of foul-smelling asafetida, hoping to ward off the frequently fatal illness. Harley's company did not escape; all of them, it seemed, were sick at one time or another, and Leslie Van Court, their very popular leading man, died at the peak of the epidemic. The actors huddled around their stoves, tried to stretch their dwindling resources, and waited for the coming of spring.

In March of 1919, borrowing the name of the theatre in which they had closed, Sadler's "Liberty Players" opened at the Home Theatre in nearby Hutchinson. The engagement was apparently successful, the company remaining there until the second week of May.

Returning to Wichita, the young manager unpacked the Brunk's No. 1 tent and reopened on the same lot he had occupied the previous fall. People were hungry for entertainment after passage of the terrible winter, and the company was again doing SRO business. In fact, attendance was so good that he remained at the Wichita location until September, awaiting Glen's return from overseas.

Ten months after the Armistice had been signed, Corporal Glen Brunk came home from France to find his show prospering in the same location where he had left it. Taking charge again, this second eldest of the Brunk brothers started out on a tour through his old Oklahoma territory.

Not surprisingly, Harley was no longer content to be a mere employee. According to Henry L. (Hank) Brunk, Glen's youngest brother,

Harley decided he wanted his own show to manage, so Glen, realizing the talent that Harley had, didn't want him to get away.

While in Wichita, Harley had gotten an old Allen automobile, so Glen bought it from Harley for $500. Then Glen loaned him $500, making $1000. Glen put in another $1000 and L.D. Brunk of Nowata, Oklahoma, who was an uncle of the Brunk boys, put in another $1000. With the $3000 and plenty of good Brunk credit in Kansas City, the No. 3 Brunks' Comedians was launched. The No. 1 show belonged to Glen, and the No. 2 show belonged to Fred Brunk. Hence the No. 3 show with Harley Sadler as "Manager and Equal Owner." Harley always said the reason he called his show the No. 3 show was because it did three times the business of the other two shows.

The third Brunk company opened that autumn in Davis, Oklahoma. Harley was ill and missed his own grand opening, causing him to say in later years that Billie and actor Marv Landrum had been with the show longer than he. However, the newly independent manager quickly recovered, heading his show for the Texas Panhandle and the towns he had toured with Roy E. Fox. As Fox had done so profitably, he decided to stay out for the entire winter.

His show was an immediate success, and the size of his audiences was little short of phenomenal. "I really believe that Sadler would do business on the Sahara Desert," a visiting performer wrote to *Billboard*. "With cotton a cent and a half a pound in the field and costing two cents a pound to pick it, people are in no mood for amusements or letting go a nickel unless absolutely necessary." Nevertheless, the writer testified, Brunks No. 3 was packing them in.

In 1921, an advance agent for Honest Bill's Circus caught the Sadler show in the Texas Panhandle and sent the following account to *Billboard*:

On July 23 I was booking Tulia, Texas, where Brunks' No. 3 was playing a return date. Wish to state that the public demanded Harley Sadler, manager, to give two night performances, and both houses were packed to capacity. Mr. Sadler is a real fellow, well met, and an entertainer both on and off stage. He is surrounded with a company far above average.

A young Harley, in a dramatic (and uncharacteristic) pose.

Business has been wonderful, and the show deserves it, for it is giving the public a real show.

A few weeks later, *Billboard* carried the following story, further evidence of Sadler's unbelievable popularity:

The following bonafide testimonial, in the form of a hand bill, was given by the citizens of Memphis, Texas, to Brunks' No. 3 show, of which Harley Sadler is manager. "In consideration of the clean, high-class shows given the past week in our city, we, the citizens of Memphis (Tex.), wish to show our appreciation for such entertainment by recommending this show to the people of Clarendon. You'll find nothing offensive in any show presented by Brunks' Comedians. We do this purely in appreciation of the excellent show presented in Memphis, and without the knowledge or consent of the manager of the above mentioned show."

Financial records from the 1921 season, recently donated to Texas Tech University's Southwest Collection by Joe McKennon, reveal just how prosperous Harley's first solo flight as manager proved to be. As a member of the company, Harley paid himself only $50 weekly, his wife drawing a modest $35. As a partner, however, he shared equally with L.D. Brunk in the profits of the organization, which were considerable. The records for the five months contained in this ledger (May through September) show that the highest monthly gross attained was $10,244.71, and that the largest monthly net profit was $3,647.06. Average monthly profit was only $1,902, but this resulted largely from a dismal showing for the month of June, which had a total credit of only $76.92. Newspaper accounts from the Texas Panhandle, where the show was playing, reveal that the area was awash with torrential rains which left wheat fields and highways flooded—and rendered dirt roads all but impassable. Hailstorms and tornadoes added to the weather woes of the region.

Expenses were heavy on the Brunk-Sadler show: three years after the ending of the hostilities in Europe, a "war tax" still siphoned off more than 11½% of the gross revenue; operating expenses (which included a $600 payroll) ran to more than $1,000 weekly; payments for the new tent in which the company performed totalled $1,888.

Nevertheless, profits for that day and age were astounding. With a company of less than twenty being paid an average salary of thirty-five dollars, (an advertisement in the *Randall County News* claims "30-PEOPLE-30," but this is publicity puffery) Sadler was well on the way to making a million dollars.

At the end of 1921, a three year contract which Harley had signed with Glen Brunk came to an end. The $500 loan from Glen which had helped to begin Brunks' #3 was repaid, and Harley was wealthy enough to buy out Uncle L.D.'s share of the partnership. Amicably, the Brunks and the Sadlers severed business connections. The two families remained fast friends—even if they did maintain a friendly rivalry. Their shows crisscrossed much of the same territory, and while they competed strenuously for audiences, there was little of the throat-cutting that sometimes characterized box office battles. Once, for example, when Henry Brunk found Sadler's advance men lying beside a country road too full of moonshine to put up the show's "paper," Henry turned out his own crew to put up posters for the competition.

By 1922, the thirty-year-old Sadler had his own show free and clear. He could, with a certain amount of pride, point to the banner over his box office which proclaimed independence. It read,

HARLEY SADLER'S OWN SHOW.

Chapter Three

On the Road: Wink, Waco, Waxahachie

AS WITH MOST TENT SHOW owner/operators, Harley
developed a touring pattern which remained more or less
constant during the good years. Basically it was seasonal,
beginning in March at such south-central Texas towns as
Waco and Brownwood, proceeding northward to the upper
limits of the Texas Panhandle as the weather warmed. A
week's stand was usual, but the stay could be lengthened to
as long as two months in occasional larger cities.

Early spring can be chilly, even in Texas, so the tent was
double sidewalled, with a "mud flap" buried in the soil to
keep drafts from feet and ankles. Several stoves were spaced
around the interior, their flue pipes snaking out through
wooden panels set in the sidewalls. Coke, a refined version of
coal, was used as fuel in the earliest heaters, which were little
more than pits dug in the earth and covered with half an oil
drum. Gradually, these crude "salamanders" gave way to
more sophisticated heaters using kerosene or oil as fuel.
Although tent fires were not uncommon, surprisingly few
occurred during the seasons when heaters were being used.
Henry Brunk tells of one occasion when his actors in a
heated tent began passing out from oxygen starvation, but
he was quick-witted enough to open a flap before any
permanent harm was done. There are no records of any
asphyxiation taking place in buttoned-up tents, but
unexplained headaches were probably not uncommon.

Warmer weather brought the troupe slowly northward
to such far Western Texas towns as Monahans, Odessa,
Kermit and El Paso, then across the New Mexico border to
play dates in Carlsbad, Hobbs, Clovis, and Roswell. Summer
days in these semi-desert regions can be blistering hot, but
the temperature drops rapidly as the sun sinks below the
horizon. With the sidewalls raised, a tent will cool rapidly
from the heat of the day. Harley experimented with
washtubs full of ice set under stage, fans wafting the cooling

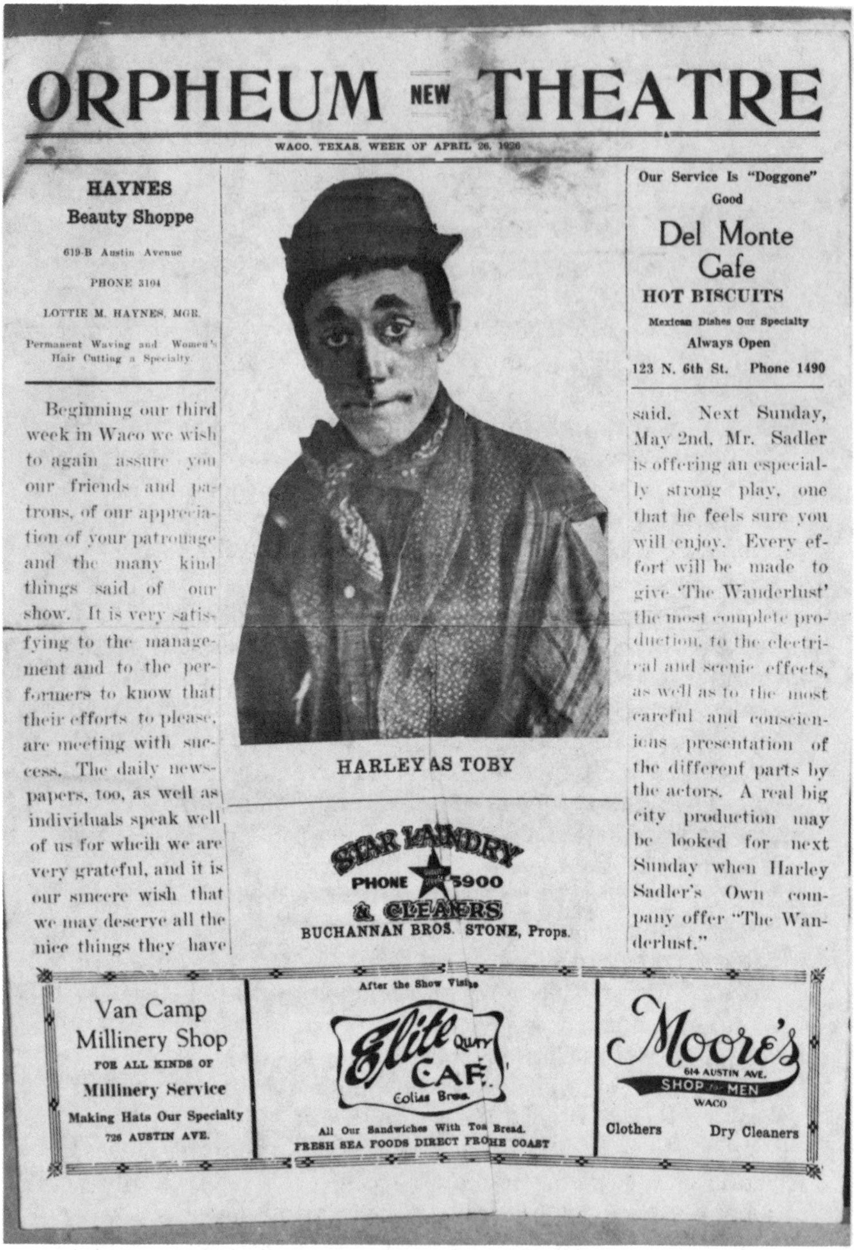

ORPHEUM NEW THEATRE

WACO, TEXAS, WEEK OF APRIL 26, 1926

HAYNES
Beauty Shoppe
619-B Austin Avenue
PHONE 3104
LOTTIE M. HAYNES, MGR.
Permanent Waving and Women's Hair Cutting a Specialty

Beginning our third week in Waco we wish to again assure you our friends and patrons, of our appreciation of your patronage and the many kind things said of our show. It is very satisfying to the management and to the performers to know that their efforts to please, are meeting with success. The daily newspapers, too, as well as individuals speak well of us for wheih we are very grateful, and it is our sincere wish that we may deserve all the nice things they have said. Next Sunday, May 2nd, Mr. Sadler is offering an especially strong play, one that he feels sure you will enjoy. Every effort will be made to give 'The Wanderlust' the most complete production, to the electrical and scenic effects, as well as to the most careful and conscienicus presentation of the different parts by the actors. A real big city production may be looked for next Sunday when Harley Sadler's Own company offer "The Wanderlust."

HARLEY AS TOBY

Our Service Is "Doggone" Good
Del Monte Cafe
HOT BISCUITS
Mexican Dishes Our Specialty
Always Open
123 N. 6th St. Phone 1490

STAR LAUNDRY
PHONE 5900
& CLEANERS
BUCHANNAN BROS. STONE, Props.

Van Camp Millinery Shop
FOR ALL KINDS OF
Millinery Service
Making Hats Our Specialty
726 AUSTIN AVE.

After the Show Visit
Elite Quality Cafe
Colias Bros.
All Our Sandwiches With Toa[st] Bread.
FRESH SEA FOODS DIRECT FRO[M T]HE COAST

Moore's
614 AUSTIN AVE.
SHOP for MEN
WACO
Clothers Dry Cleaners

During the winter months—and sometimes into the late spring, Harley and a smaller company played the regular, indoor theatres.

air over the audience, but this proved only psychologically beneficial. There were undoubtedly some uncomfortably warm—and cold—performances done under canvas, but this was a different time, with different standards of comfort. In days before central heating and air conditioning, people seemed more tolerant of the extremes of temperature; and actors called upon to do a matinee of *Call of the Woods*, uncomplainingly donned furs and woolens to perform in the broiling heat of a summer afternoon.

By autumn of a usual year, the company would be playing on the Texas High Plains, hoping that a good harvest had left farm families with at least a few extra coins jingling in their overalls. Then, as the winds of fall brought a chill—and sometimes snow—to the region, the company began a southward retreat, ending the year's tour with a traditional Yuletide banquet in San Angelo.

The tent, thoroughly dried and liberally sprinkled with black pepper to discourage residence by mice and crickets, was carefully stored with the rest of the equipment in a vacant barn rented from a local farmer. For most of the company, winter was not a time for rest and relaxation. As soon as the Christmas holidays were behind, Harley organized a stock company to play the indoor theatres. The troupe, reduced in size from the summer aggregation, sometimes played stands of several weeks in such larger cities as Houston, San Antonio or Fort Worth. In less populated areas, a "circle stock" pattern was followed, performing one night a week in six towns located on the circumference of a wheel. This was a very common touring arrangement for companies during the twenties: while one play was being performed at night, the following week's offering was being rehearsed in the daytime. Thus, after a six nights' run—with Sunday dark—the actors were ready to retrace the circle with a new presentation. This routine would be repeated until audiences began to dwindle. Stock was more sober, more conventionally dramatic, lacking the circus hoopla and excitement that was so much a part of rag-top performances. Gone was the candy pitch, the marching band, and much of the vaudeville.

But as soon as the first southern breezes brought a hint of spring to Texas, the company would be swarming over the barn where the summer's theatre was stored. The tent would be unpacked—to a chorus of sneezes as black pepper filled the air—and the inevitable rips were mended and missing grommets replaced. Chairs and bleachers were given needed repairs, scenery was painted. As work on the equipment proceeded, actors began rehearsing their opening bill of six shows. At the end of a week, the show opened a new season. The actors may have been a little shaky in their lines, the vaudeville a little under-rehearsed, and the scenery incomplete, but the economics of the situation did not allow for more than a week of non-revenue producing preparation.

The tent shows, Sadler's included, were mainly a village phenomenon. In a letter to *Billboard*, Harley remarked that his type of entertainment was generally restricted to towns of less than ten thousand. No crossroads settlements were too small to attract a traveling tent company. Through the twenties and early thirties, a show playing in the hinterlands could probably count on drawing audiences from no more than a fifteen mile radius, given the deeply rutted dirt roads and undependable automobiles. The plays needed to come to the populace; thus such entertainment-starved West Texas villages as Spur, Dickens, Matador, Slaton, Justiceburg, and the now-vanished Tuxedo ("TUCKsy-doe") provided excellent box office returns. An often-told story, probably true in its essentials, has a recently hired actor from the East standing outside a tent, looking disdainfully across the vacant West Texas plains. All that disturbed his view of the unbroken horizon was a "town" consisting of a general store, blacksmith shop, and three houses clustered at the intersection of two single-lane dirt roads.

"Where," the newcomer disdainfully asked a grizzled canvasman sitting cross-legged on the ground, "Where do they expect to get an audience to fill this tent?"

The old-timer looked up from a piece of sidewall he was mending with a sailmaker's palm and needle, spat in the dust beside him, and snorted his reply: "You just wait 'til long about dark, young feller, and you'll see lanterns and buggy lights come a-winkin' from all over like a hull swarm of lightnin' bugs."

A certain amount of pre-arrival publicity was necessary to assure a full tent, but by present-day standards, the quantity was astonishingly little. Word-of-mouth was the best form of advertising, and news of this forthcoming major event in the social life of the community spread with the speed of a prairie fire.

Ferd, the youngest Sadler brother, worked as advance man through much of the twenties, usually arriving in town only two or three days before the show train was scheduled.

In the 20's, even such small communities as Spur provided audiences for a week's stand.

Although a general route would be roughed out at the beginning of a season, the itinerary sometimes changed from day to day: a drought, a snowstorm, conflicting dates with the circus or a barnstorming evangelist, a railroad bridge washout—any number of variables could abruptly head the troupe in a different direction. Generally, however, Harley tended to repeat towns year after year, having about sixty favored playing locations and appearing at thirty of these in a season. "It was always a pleasure to put up paper in a town we'd already been to," Ferd recalled. "I was greeted like kinfolks."

Harley's advance agent did little of the circus-inspired bill posting on barns and fences. Ferd carried a bundle of window cards when he stepped off the train at the little wooden depot; stopping only long enough to drop his valise at a familiar hotel or boarding house, he would begin his trip down the main street of the town. Bearing an unmistakable resemblance to his famous older brother, Ferd would howdy and shake his way from one business establishment to another, leaving one or two cards in each store front. Merchants were always ready to put up a Sadler ad, even without the complimentary tickets that Ferd thrust upon them. "Be free with the comps, expecially for Monday night opening," the advance man was instructed, and he was always happy to comply. Even the barber, who jealously guarded the natural light that came in through his plate glass window, usually found room for one of Harley's posters.

While Ferd was getting a shave, he would occasionally pick up rumors of opposition from the local moving picture man; but for the most part, the manager of the "flickers" seldom risked direct confrontation with the popular showman. Putting on his bravest smile, the celluloid entrepreneur would take his family to the Sadler tent on the passes provided him—knowing that while he sat "enjoying" the show, his movie was playing to perhaps a dozen people. He might wax as morally indignant as he wished with some poor, rag-topped "Tom" show which happened to light in his town, but Harley's show was untouchable, in the same class as Mother and The Flag.

Ferd's next stop after the barber shop was the newspaper office, where he placed large ads for the following week. He was generally successful in promoting a feature story or two about the coming of the Sadler troupe.

He would then call on the president of whatever

organization was to sponsor the show's appearance. Typically, the American Legion, Shriners, VFW, Lions, or volunteer fire department was overjoyed to provide the three "L's" (lot, license, and 'lectricity) in exchange for ten percent of the gross ticket sales for the week. Costs of these were small. Frequently use of the lot was donated—or owned by Sadler himself—the license fee was often remitted by the town council, and electricity for the week might run to twenty-five dollars. In exchange for very little in the way of service or expenditure, the sponsor would amass several hundred dollars for the treasury. Expensive though the 10% might be (in 1927, sponsorship cost Harley the small fortune of $7,456) this system had the virtue of allying him with a reputable local organization. Thus, any attack upon the Sadler show became also an attack upon a prominent group of local citizens.

Along his route, the youngest of the Sadler clan would pick up several requests for free entertainment. There was usually a noontime Rotary program (Harley was a member with a long record of perfect attendance), a church social, a fund-raiser for the hospital or for new band uniforms, a civic celebration of one sort or another. Ferd accepted all invitations to perform, assuring whoever asked that Harley would have some of his troupe there, and would try to appear himself.

A Saturday afternoon baseball game needed to be scheduled, usually with the local champion. Baseball was one of Harley's passions, and at one time he owned the Stamford franchise in the Texas league. Harve Holland's Comedians, another Texas show, made it a practice to lose gracefully to local teams, even the Boy Scouts, but Harley was dead serious about putting up the best possible team. And winning! Rolland Haverstock, who had grown up on his family's show and seemed destined to follow his father into the major leagues, recalls that he was hired on the Sadler show as much for his shortstopping ability as any other talent. Paul Thardo-Kalmbacher, even when he was playing drums on other shows, would frequently "job in" for an afternoon of baseball wearing the Sadler uniform—catching the milk train after his company's Friday night show, playing ball on Saturday, then taking the evening train back to his own company, arriving barely in time for the Saturday night show.

As one of his tasks, Ferd often had to superintend the mailing of hundreds of COMING NEXT WEEK penny postcards to rural mailboxes. Sometimes he could sweet-talk the central operator into allowing him to make party line announcements from the local telephone exchange. One way or another, word of the show's imminent arrival spread rapidly.

The people of the area began preparations for play-going. Attire was informal, but even informality has certain sartorial requirements, especially for young adults in their courting years. Aside from new items of clothing, money had to be found for tickets, popcorn, shaved ice, and prize candy. Few household budgets could provide six nights' admission money for a large family unless some rigid economies were taken before the show arrived—and after it had departed.

The luckiest people in town were those with passes for the entire week. All local dignitaries automatically received these prized ducats: mayor, town council, police chief, ministers, school superintendents together with their families were automatically "complimented" when Sadler was in town. Aside from the tickets which Ferd had liberally bestowed on his advance rounds, Harley himself was generous in handing out comps to friends and acquaintances. For a few years, the openhanded manager followed the custom of giving lifetime passes, small wallet-sized metal cards, to particular friends, but this proved ultimately too expensive. All Sadler audiences were liberally sprinkled with free admissions, a practice which cut into box office receipts, but which was defended as a means of generating good will.

Paying customers frequently had to scramble to raise admission money, usually 25¢ for adults and 15¢ for children. The Sadler show was not to be missed under any circumstances. For weeks after, conversations would begin with something like, "Hey, you remember when that quartet sang, with ole Harley not knowin' what the words were?" Anyone who didn't remember found himself excluded from a lot of conversations. "In those days," recalls Maurice Brookes, an Abilene lawyer, "all there was in those towns was the Church, the Masonic Lodge, and Harley Sadler."

All the travelling shows tended to follow the harvest, for if crops were good, admission money was plentiful. During the year, ready cash was a rare commodity for most farm families, but after threshing or picking, when the bill at the store had been paid off and the loan at the bank reduced a few hundred dollars or so, after winter clothes and school supplies had been purchased, some money was usually left over for celebrating.

Salaried townspeople perhaps had a little more money than their country cousins, but parents did not dispense dollar bills with today's casualness. Children were expected to earn their amusement funds, and not a few town boys paid for their Sadler admissions by picking cotton. Many housewives, both in the town and the country, carefully counted the coins that collected in the ornamental sugar bowl sitting high on a top shelf, and considered selling a hen or two from the laying flock.

Some of the worldly town boys (unfortunate children who had grown up with pavement rather than dirt beneath their feet) would sometimes charge a watermelon to their father's grocery store account, then sell it on the street for half price in order to get ticket money. One way or another, most of the county contrived to get ticket money. Ferd recalled remarking once to a furniture store owner in Santa Anna that the town looked a little quiet. "Don't you worry none," the owner snorted in reply. "Folks around here would sell their furniture to see *Harley's* show."

Ferd was in the furniture store that day to see about borrowing properties for the show, another of his duties to be performed before the show arrived. Harley traveled with little beyond the bare walls of a setting, knowing that he would have his choice of furnishings from several of the town's living rooms and many of the stores. Borrowing cost him only a few passes and a mention of the store during his curtain speech. Even a baby would be lent to the show if a script called for one, and none of the actors had a child of suitable size. Once a borrowed baby was followed onstage by the family dog, used to walking beside the carriage. The myriad little boys who sat near the stage looked at the dog, drew the obvious conclusion, and hooted derision: "That's not the lady's child! That's the Mixson's baby!"

Ferd's assignments were completed by Saturday, giving him a day off with little to do but attend three worship programs (Sunday school, morning services, evening services) and await the arrival of the show train early Monday morning; God, weather, and the railroads willing. Put-up day saw Harley's gaudily painted baggage and passenger cars arrive on a downtown siding, propelled by a smoke-belching little switch engine. Local draymen, alerted by the advance agent, were waiting with wagons to begin moving the masses of equipment to the show lot. From the baggage car spilled forth heavy bundles of canvas, poles,

Cowboy plays were standard fare in the Southwest.

A typical help wanted advertisement from Billboard, in 1927. Versatility was essential.

coiled ropes, stakes,marquee, lights, wardrobe, bleachers, chairs, scenery, ticket booth, stage platforming, curtains—a bewildering mass of equipment to be moved and set in place for the opening performance that night.

From the passenger car emerged the actors and actresses, parading with studied casualness before hundreds of goggle-eyed towners who had come down to welcome them. Each performer carried a small suitcase (the hotel trunk would follow later), with possibly a little dog on a leash or a canary in a cage. If the weather was chilly, a coal oil heater would be part of their equipment. These evil-smelling portable furnaces, about thirty inches high and a foot in diameter, were often fancifully slip-covered by the costume ladies of the company. Central heating was still a novelty during the twenties, and these little stoves were necessary to an actor's survival. Not only would they keep sleeping rooms habitable, they could warm a backstage or a railroad car, heat wash water or a smoothing iron—and cook a meal if the week's salary was running a little short. Pot-bellied stoves kept hotel parlors and dining rooms at a comfortable temperature, but rooms removed from these sources were often near freezing. Henry Brunk tells of a member of his company who came down to the hotel lobby one night to warm himself shortly after the local doctor had returned from an emergency call in the country. The actor looked in amazement at the snow-flecked physician huddled near the brick-red stove, icicles on his beard just beginning to melt and drip water onto the carpet. "Good lord, man," said the actor, "what room have they got you in?"

The company's first stroll through the town was an important event, and performers always chose their spiffiest outfits. "Dress well on and off (stage)" was a frequent requirement found in *Billboard* advertisements for actors, and the successful ones spent a great deal of time and money on their wardrobes. For the ladies of the town, the daytime attire of the actors provided as much grist for the conversation mills as the evening's entertainment at the tent.

Fashion critics kept their sharpest eye out for Billie Sadler, who dressed simply but in the very height of Texas style. The popular wife of the company manager/owner could not help but be aware of her position as leader of fashion, and responded by spending endless hours in dress shops, looking for "just the right" blouse, or scarf, or earrings. Although most of her clothing came from boutiques in the major cities, her taste was discerning enough that she could sometimes find what she wanted in a small town Woolworth's. "Of course," one of her admirers sighed, "Billie was the kind of woman who would look good in a potato sack with a rope around the middle."

For the Singer-clad ladies who ordered patterns from the latest Monkey Ward catalogue and cut their dresses from feed-sack prints, Billie Sadler walking down Main Street was as much of a fashion show as they were ever to witness. Even today, women who lived along the Sadler route-of-march can describe in great detail "what Billie had on" at a particular moment: in the dry goods store, at church, in the candy kitchen after the show.

Since most of the towns played were return engagements, the company could expect warm greetings from friends they had made in past years. After moving into familiar rooms at a boarding house or hotel, the actors would spread out through the town to pick up threads of life which had been interrupted by their departure the previous year.

Actresses of the company wasted little time in descending upon the local stores, where they made good their manager's boast that his people "didn't buy out of the catalogue," and weren't "taking all the money out of town," as the movie manager so often implied. The married men headed for the barber shop to catch up on the latest happenings around town, while the single ones began phoning girls they had dated the last time around. Some of the smaller children would be farmed out to local families. Sue Kelley, wife of the boss canvasman, recalls that her two small daughters were virtually kidnapped by friends at each town they played, to be returned in well-scrubbed, well-entertained, and moderately overfed condition when time came to depart.

Harley collected a crowd wherever he went. After a quick round of handshakes at the railroad siding, he would sprint to the show lot to check the positioning of the tent. Placement of the marquee and front door, he always felt, had a great influence on the attendance. By the time he arrived, the sidewalk around the lot would be ringed with small boys desperately hoping for a "Hey you, boy, grab some of them chairs and carry 'em inside." Work meant a pass for the week, and a chance to bask in reflected glory that came from rubbing elbows with the glamorous tent show people. "I helped Harley put up the tent this morning," a father would be told by a proud ten-year-old that evening when he came home from work.

While the actors were getting reacquainted around the town, the canvas crews were hard at work, intent on raising their stately pleasure dome in time to get a hot supper before the evening performance. The stage had to be erected, bleachers assembled, dressing rooms set up. As the canvas was spread out and sections laced together, gangs of three or four men swinging heavy sledgehammers, rhythmically drove wooden stakes into the soil. Other crews raised the centerpoles and guyed them out: at a signal, everyone turned-to, joined in hoisting the bale-rings to the tops of the poles.

If the train arrived on time, put-up was a leisurely and orderly process, but the crews had to scurry when the railroad ran behind schedule. Tension could be felt in the air, with shouted instructions flying back and forth. But no swearing! Harley didn't want any of the small fry setting up chairs and bleachers to learn any new words to carry home. A mashed thumb might rate a "Gol-Dernit" but that was the limit of the rough talk from the crews.

Harley made the crews nervous. He tended to fuss, to wonder whether the stakes would hold, whether a guy rope was too tight or too loose. Claude Kelley, his capable canvasman, once in a fit of exasperation told his employer to go back to the hotel and let the crews do the work. Harley went.

Leaving the lot, the show manager would stroll downtown. Everywhere he was regarded as a favorite son, and he managed to convey the impression that this particular town was one of his very special favorites. His memory for names and faces was incredible and nearly infallible. In a hundred towns he could stand on a street corner and greet people by name.

"Hello, J.B.," he'd say to a local merchant whom he hadn't seen for a year. "Your boy get out the hospital? He feeling all right?"

"Why Minnie Lou," he would say to a familiar face behind the drug store counter, "Have you heard from your daughter? How does she like it up North?"

In late afternoon, the young manager would break off from the crowd of people surrounding him and journey back to the now-erected tent. There, members of his all-male band would be changing into their marching uniforms for the concert on the town square. In later years, Harley's band appeared in cowboy costumes with ten gallon hats, but during the twenties, they wore semi-military dress with riding boots, brass buttons and plumes. A profusion of gold braid meandered around the sleeves and across the chest. Sadler had given up the trombone in favor of an enormous brass drum, a change which allowed him to howdy the spectators along the line of march. His greetings did little for the tempo of the band, however, which found itself constantly out of step and off beat. "Harley," said a cornet player one day, "You've just got to hire another man for the band, either someone to wave at the people or someone to beat that derned drum. *Because you cain't do both!*"

An excellent account of Harley's downtown concert has been left by O.A. Peterson, the same literate musician who recorded the Roy E. Fox blowdown for *Billboard*. In 1921, while visiting the Sadler show (still operating under the Brunk banner), Peterson penned the following for the Repertoire page of *Billboard*:

They give a concert uptown on opening day only. Each evening they play in front of the tent where the show is located—never uptown where the drink stores and picture house are. Sadler says: "While I have a band I might as well use it for the benefit of the show." A wise logic.

Each manager presented a "ballyhoo" as part of the uptown concert, a brief speech in which he extolled the virtues of his company and hinted at the many delights awaiting the spectators. Harley's was always a very modest statement. Unstrapping his bass drum he stepped to the front of his band and spoke in the deep, resonant voice which never failed to surprise people expecting a high tenor to come from that slight frame. Peterson continues:

He is a likable fellow. He has a real man's voice which he uses in a pleasing manner. He talks in a conversational tone, never in the raucous, ponderous style assumed by most spielers. Neither does he assume the patronizing tone nor the broad smile of undue familiarity. He tells them about his show in a quiet, modest, unassuming manner, but with evident sincerity. Then he steps behind his bass drum, they play another tune and the crowd is his from then on.

Forming into marching order, the band paraded back to the tent, doing its best to keep step with an ever-erratic drummer. Little boys fell in behind, walking with giant steps to match the stride of the band. Trailing the band, hundreds of spectators began to move toward the tent, many of the men already reaching for the leather purses which

Advertisement for a long run in Austin, around 1930.

The Sadler street band, in the early 20's.

contained their ticket money. Laughing and talking excitedly, the crowd moved into the tent, anxious to get good seats.

Curtain in fifteen minutes!

Chapter Four

"DRAMA, MUSIC, VAUDEVILLE:
America's BIGGEST and BEST
TRAVELING STOCK COMPANY
Appearing in the Largest and Most Elaborate
Tent Theatre Ever Built."

WHEN APPLIED TO SHOW BUSINESS, such superlatives as "biggest," "best," "largest" and "most" are more than a little suspect. Whether Harley fully deserved the magniloquent billing he bestowed upon his enterprise in the mid-thirties is a matter open to discussion. If Sadler did not perch at the absolute pinnacle of the several thousand shows touring under canvas, he certainly had as legitimate a claim to the honor as any other. According to Rolland Haverstock, who grew up on his family's show touring North Texas and Oklahoma, "Harley Sadler was what we called the cream of the crop. He was class. The rest of us ... well, you couldn't tell our shows apart." Professor William Slout, whose childhood was spent on the Michigan circuit, remembers the near-awe with which the Midwest managers discussed this mammoth attraction: like everything else in Texas, Sadler's show loomed larger than life.

Undoubtedly the Southwestern showman enjoyed a national reputation, but one restricted to the readers of the Tent Repertoire pages of *Billboard*. Except for his fellow performers throughout the nation, the Sadler name was virtually unknown outside his two-state touring area of Texas and Eastern New Mexico. This limited fame was a natural result of the tent show's efforts to appeal to a limited, specific, and intensely regional clientele.

While the nation-spanning theatrical syndicates were searching frantically for an ever-lowering common denominator of public appetite, one enabling them to produce plays which would appeal equally to Massachusetts, Mobile and Mulberry Grove, the rag opries

63

were concerning themselves with scripts that were adapted to a local situation. Actors spoke in the dialect of their audience, not in the London West End accent which Broadway actors regarded as the only proper speech for the stage. Thus, these shows were better able to satisfy the dramatic appetites of a particular folk than were the major producing organizations operating out of New York.

The typical big city fare of comedy-dramas about ritzy society swells living on the Eastern Seaboard had very little meaning for people living in the hinterlands; and they were easily scandalized by the sexual innuendo of high comedy and the lusty romps of bedroom farce. These unsophisticated audiences wanted characters and situations with which they could easily identify, an unending parade of stock dramatic situations which were as fixed and unchanging as much of today's television. Problem dramas were acceptable, but they had to concern themselves with problems that could be handled without a great deal of mental agitation. A moral dilemma could be presented only if the neat solution by the final curtain was reached through the generous application of such homely virtues as charity, chastity, forgiveness, conformity, and (above all) Christian love. While Broadway was cranking out naughty comedies and girlie revues for the tired businessman, the tent theatre was producing rural comedies and moral dramas for the tired ranchers and farmers—and their equally exhausted families.

One of the clearest pictures of the Sadler show in its heyday is that retained by Louise Hefner. Louise is now Mrs. George Sorensen, Sr., but some fifty years ago she was identified only as the daughter of Faye Moore, a beautiful actress who had married A.C. Hefner, one of Harley's most popular performers. As a child, Louise spent the school year with her stepfather's parents in Kansas, but the summers of 1921-25 were for her, holiday time on the road.

After a winter of drab ordinariness in a little Kansas town, summers were like vacations in fairyland, where she became the child of the glamorous leading lady, and where her newfound father was the handsome, blue-eyed leading man who huffed so comically on the tuba in the street band. ("Hef" or "Ace" wore a toupee to hide his premature baldness, and delighted in whipping if off in the barber's chair when the barber's back was turned.) Gloria Sadler, crown princess of the Sadler dynasty, was also on the show during this time, and provided a playmate for the young girl.

As might be expected, Louise went on the stage, helping to supply that indispensible ingredient of every vaudeville entertainment, the performing child. There has never been a time in popular entertainment when a wide-eyed, innocent-looking little girl has not been greeted by a maternal chorus of "Oooooh!" when she stepped on the stage. "I was," Mrs. Sorensen remembers with a self-deprecating smile, "a prissy little girl who could sing and dance." She appeared in specialty dances like the Charleston and Black Bottom—and received a salary, like the rest of the company. Harley himself made a point of asking the treasurer for a ten dollar bill, presenting it to the tiny performer "with great ceremony."

On the road, Louise's day typically began before the rest of the company was stirring. Actors are essentially night people. Their working hours begin in the evening, and they are seldom ready for bed until several hours after final curtain, when the exhiliration of performance has faded. Louise's parents were typical, seldom appearing on the scene until the sun had begun its descent in the heavens. On most mornings, the young girl would slip from her bed in the family's room, dress quietly and tiptoe to the door, pausing to pick up the breakfast money that was always left on the dresser top. Except for the children and a few compulsive sun-greeters, the company began stirring around noon, dressing leisurely and going down to the restaurant for their first meal of the day.

In these halcyon days when the company usually numbered between fifty and sixty, work was dispersed enough that everyone had a fair amount of leisure time. Unless a new script was being rehearsed or an act added to the vaudeville, actors were free during the afternoons to shop, visit, write letters, or see to their wardrobes.

Costuming for both stage and street took a great deal of time. Harley insisted that his actors appear neat and clean at all times. There were to be no ravelings or drooping hemlines, no baggy trousers, no stains or wrinkles. In these days before no-iron materials and corner laundromats, clothing care consumed endless hours. A pleated shirtwaist, for example, needed to be scrubbed with bar soap, rinsed, wrung out, dipped in blueing, and hung out to dry. Starch was then dissolved in water, stirred and boiled to smooth consistency, finally diluted to various strengths to be used on different parts of the garment. After starching and drying once again, the shirtwaist was dampened, rolled tightly, and allowed to rest overnight, to be ironed the following day with a heavy instrument heated on the stove. Usually one day's wearing was all that could be accomplished before dust, dirt and the soot from cooking and heating fires made another washing necessary. Many single men eased their cleaning problems by wearing celluloid collars and cuffs which could be "washed" with a pencil eraser.

Actors were also responsible for their own stage costumes, and most of them travelled with several wardrobe trunks, never knowing what role might befall in the course of the season. Not all, of course, were equipped for every eventuality, and the excuse, "I'm sorry, but I left that costume in my other trunk" was heard so often that some managers, in telegraphing a new actor to join the show, would routinely add, "BRING OTHER TRUNK." Roy E. Fox, in one of his *Billboard* articles, wrote of a young replacement actor who appeared onstage in a light summer suit while a blizzard was supposed to be howling outside the door. When the irate manager collared the new performer after curtain, he was told with total ingenuousness, "Well, you see, Mr. Fox, I didn't have a winter overcoat with me, so I put on *two suits of long underwear!*"

Louise Hefner generally escaped these wardrobe chores, spending the afternoon playing with Gloria if not performing that night, taking a hated afternoon nap if she was. After the evening meal, she would go to the tent location with her parents. While they were making up, she often wandered around to the front of the house to talk with the lady in the brightly-painted box office cubicle. Above them, swaying in the slight breeze, was a large banner proclaiming HARLEY SADLER COMEDIANS, framed on the sides of fluttering pennants. Sandwich boards displaying pictures of the performers sat out front of the tent when weather was pleasant. If thunderheads lowered on the horizon, the boards were moved to the small lobby which contained a popcorn machine and other concessions.

After pausing for a moment to greet the lady manning the ticket box at a canvas archway, the young girl passed into the main tent, where seats were already beginning to fill. The cheaper, general admission area was in the rear bleachers, usually called the "blues" because of the circus custom of painting cheaper seats in that color. (The name usually applied by the town boys was "buzzard's roost.")

Toward the stage, a low wooden fence separated the

"reserved seats" from the rest. Another ticket-catcher was stationed at an opening in the wooden divider, to collect an additional charge from those who wanted a closer-up view from a somewhat more comfortable seat. These slip-covered, unpadded chairs were reserved in name only, seating being on a first-come basis. Late in the twenties, however, Sadler did add a few rows of genuinely reserved seats, leatherette director's chairs which could be purchased in advance at a downtown drugstore or cigar stand.

Tents were more than substitutes for real theatres. In a pre-airconditioning age, a tent with its sidewalls rolled up could be comfortably cool shortly after sundown on a scorching summer's evening—at a time when a regular theatre would feel like the inside of a furnace. The canvas dome suggested a relaxed, neighborly experience, possessed an ambience at the opposite pole of a starchy, dress-up "cultural" evening. Louise's strongest memory is one of "playtime," of men in shirt sleeves, women in cotton dresses, grandparents, children, babies—and the inevitable stray dog. In her mind's eye, she sees everyone laughing, talking, sipping soft drinks, munching the shaved-ice cones that went with summer. "Everything shouted that this was a fun place to be."

On warm evenings the sidewalls of the tent were rolled up to allow air circulation, also providing a graceful, drapery-like swag along the bottom edge of the big-top. Bright red and blue trim helped to lend a festive air to the otherwise dull khaki-colored canvas. Stakes, poles, and ropes intersected the view in all directions—except toward the stage.

When filled to bulging capacity, Sadler's tent during this period would seat two thousand; but if more room was needed, a second side wall would be set up six feet outside the tent perimeter. Spectators would bring their own sitting devices: soap boxes, buggy seats, benches, rocking chairs from the front porch. Sawdust was spread on the ground when traffic made it too dusty, or an occasional rain turned the parched soil to mud.

Standing at the rear of the reserved seat area, Louise was not quite tall enough to see the stage floor, which was raised five feet. At the front of the seating area, a six foot no-man's-land separated the stage from the first row; any closer seating would mean stiff necks for the spectators who would have to look upward. Sometimes this space was used for the orchestra on a large musical production, but more often was

Inside of the Sadler tent at Canyon, Texas, probably in the early '30s. The orchestra platform is visible at left. Bleachers have not been erected.

filled with small boys who had managed to slip away from their parents.

The stage opening, about thirty feet in width, was covered by a blue plush curtain which drew up a series of folds, an "Austrian" in today's drapery parlance. Sequins spelling out HARLEY SADLER'S COMEDIANS in a flowing script across the width of the curtain were framed at the sides by the glittering masks of comedy and tragedy. Harley always insisted that the front curtain have a heavy pipe in the bottom: he knew that applause would be triggered by a loud "thunk!" as the pipe hit the floor. The pipe also kept the curtain from billowing when the wind blew, a fairly common condition in West Texas.

The stage was surrounded by a profusion of advertising banners, which often seemed to overpower the onstage performance. There was no limit to the number that might appear, since each represented additional income for the show's owner and the team who had the banner concession. Usually, a favored couple handled the advertising, the pretty wife turning on her most dazzling smile as she visited the shops of the local merchants, while back at the tent, her husband frantically lettered the butcher-paper signs, rushing to have them done for Monday night's opening. Proceeds of this very profitable sideline were usually split evenly between concessionaires and the owner of the show.

At the left side of the proscenium sat the orchestra platform, usually a foot below the level of the stage. Large enough to accommodate twelve to fifteen musicians, entrance was through a curtained door cut into the canvas proscenium—which opened into the men's dressing room. A sign hanging over the piano read: "IF THE BABY CRIES, PLEASE TAKE IT TO THE REAR OF THE TENT."

Louise, standing in front of the stage, was tempted to take a shortcut backstage by going up the connecting stairs and squeezing between the curtain and canvas proscenium; but this was not allowed after the house had been opened. Instead, she ducked out the sidewall and walked to the rear of the tent, where, after passing through myriad prop boxes and trunks stored on the ground, she arrived at the backstage stairs.

Going up to stage level and crossing over to the women's dressing room, Louise found her mother and the other actresses working quietly at their pre-show tasks, talking in muted tones, since only a canvas wall separated them from the audience. Still in slips, teddies, or silk pongee makeup kimonos, they were clustered around the makeup table, sharing the small, light-bulb ringed mirrors that were never numerous enough to go around. Bright, dry rouge was painted on the lips with a small brush and smoothed with a fingertip. Beaded mascara had to be heated over the small sterno stove which sat on a corner of the table. Open wardrobe trunks (Taylor was the prized brand) were scattered here and there, stockings and undergarments peeping out of half-opened drawers. A wooden screen studded with wooden pegs was hung with a profusion of costumes that would be donned moments before going onstage: the crisp, freshly ironed look must be preserved as long as possible. An ironing board sat in the corner, however, in case any last minute touchup was necessary. A kerosene heater was used to provide warmth on cool early-season evenings, being replaced in later years by a glowing circle of red-hot wire set in the middle of a copper-colored spherical reflector. For the warm evenings of late summer, a revolving electric fan helped keep perspiration from smearing the makeup.

On the opposite side of the stage, behind the orchestra platform, sat the always-crowded men's dressing room. (Historically, male roles have outnumbered female about three to one, and the tent show maintained this disproportion.) Except for a more subdued range of costumes, the men's and women's areas were much the same. Only the better-class shows, like Sadler's, had dressing rooms on the same level as the stage: in the poorer companies, actors blinded from the stage lights had to stumble down dimly lit stairs to dirt floored cubicles for costume changes.

The atmosphere backstage, as Louise remembers it, was like that of a home occupied by a large, happy family. "As a six-year-old, I never heard anyone say, 'My hours are too long' or 'I'm working too hard.' These were men and women who loved show business... and you could feel it!"

Curtain time varied with the setting of the sun, but was usually no later than 7:45 or 8:00, since farm families needed to greet the sun's reappearance on the following morning. Ten minutes before show time, the orchestra members dressed in tuxedos and evening gowns, took their places on the left platform. O.A. Peterson, who wrote approvingly of Harley's downtown concert and ballyhoo, also approved of the way he opened the show:

His orchestra is somewhat better than average—considerably better than

The tent interior, seen from the stage. Iron buggy tires were used for houselight fixtures.

some. They do not play a half hour before the show starts, wearing out their
welcome and the patience of the audience as well. They go in just ten
minutes before the curtain rises and play an overture, just like a theatre
orchestra. No long ballyhoo for the candy sale, with the audience growing
impatient every time the orchestra renders another tune. When the
orchestra comes in it means overture and then the show.

Houselights, consisting of bare light bulbs mounted on
iron buggy tires, were dimmed as the orchestra "played the
curtain up." The stage was illuminated mainly with
footlights and overhead borders, but follow spots and some
"ante-proscenium" lights were provided. As Act One began,
Peterson noted with further approval that Harley had a fast,
well-paced show.

Although he uses some of the same plays used by other shows they seem
different and more satisfying, because they are put on with pep, attention to
details and no stage waits; no loud talking in the dressing rooms, and no
stalling by the orchestra. His actors and actresses are not wonders. They
are not better than those with other rep shows, but it is the way they work;
natural, smoothly—as tho they enjoyed it, which indeed they do.

The company's repertoire contained a variety of plays.
There were the old standards, such lachrymose classics as
Ten Nights in a Barroom, East Lynne and *East Lynn* and *St.
Elmo.* Drawn from well-read novels, they were usually
referred to as "book plays."

Many dramas with contemporary settings concerned
the redemption of a man by the love of a good woman after he
had been led astray by a bad one. Comedy was the staple
ingredient of all these plays: even *Ten Nights,* a serious
temperance drama, contained some low-comedy drunk
scenes and an improbable courtship between Sample
Switchel and the town's resident old maid.

Charles Harrison, the Shakespeare of the rag tops,
seemed to possess the magic formula for blending
seriousness and laughter. *Other People's Business* was,
according to the editor of the *Albany (Texas) News,* "a
rolicking and frolicking farce,... interspersed with pathos."
Harley approved of this blend: "Comedy is my forte," he told
a reporter in the 1920s, "but I have always wanted to have a
part in a play with dramatic moments." A barrel full of
laughs seasoned with a sprinkling of tears kept audiences
crowding into the tent.

This self-taught actor, one who had never had a lesson
in his life, was able to play a variety of roles; crooks,
politicians, policemen, top hat sophisticates, and the

misunderstood miscreant of *Saintly Hypocrites and Honest Sinners.* He was particularly successful at what was called, for obscure reasons, "G-string" parts. Possibly these crackerbarrel old man roles were so named because the high, thin voice which went with the character reminded someone of monotonous sawing on a fiddle string. Others have suggested that the wispy, white goatee, often attached to the face by wire loops over the ears, resembled the strip-teaser's ultimate modesty garment. Whatever the origin, Harley made a witty, wise and believable grandpappy while he was still in his twenties. Wearing a bald wig fringed with white hair, his chin-whiskers kept in constant motion by a shifting chew of tobacco, Harley delighted his audiences with this characterization.

Of course Toby, the comedy heart of the tent show, was his best-remembered role. Although these clownish, silly-kid roles had a certain sameness about them, they did have some variations, ranging from Sputters, the stuttering cowboy who could only talk fluently when outlining an imaginary square with his finger, to the hick farm boy in *Toby from Arkansas.* Mary Roberts, a Sweetwater chum of the Sadler's daughter, remembers,

His Toby character was always lovable and funny in his oversized shoes and red wig and overalls with one strap broken. Toby made you laugh at the start of the play but toward the end when he lost the beautiful girl to the handsome leading man only a very cold heart would have left the theatre dry-eyed.

O.A. Peterson, writing for *Billboard,* noted the naturalness of Harley's performance as Toby:

At night they come to the show to see what this boy with a man's voice can do on stage. And they see plenty. He comes on a rube kid with freckles, large blue eyes, and eye-brows high up on his forehead.* No exaggerated, silly grin, no extremely foolish mannerisms; just a natural country boy with the unsophisticated look of wonderment on his face. A rarely high-class comedian is Harley Sadler. Nothing obnoxious, nothing overdone.

Indeed, Harley's playing was so natural that the folksy editor of Albany's *"Weekly Astonisher"* had difficulty in perceiving the art behind the apparent artlessness. He wrote:

*Harley, like many Tobys, turned to a thicker, more clownish makeup as he grew older in an effort to hid the lines of age.

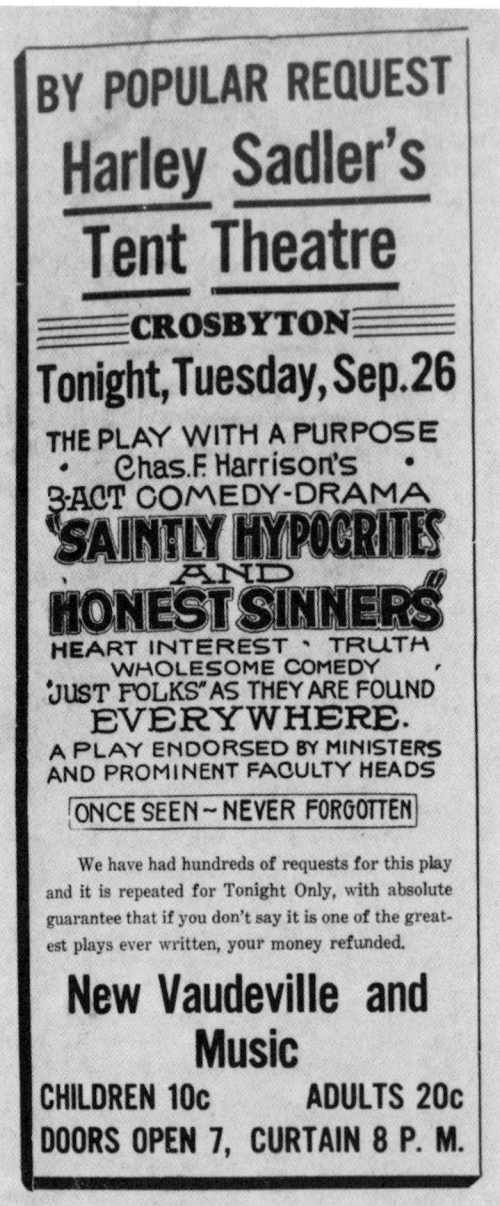

Saintly Hypocrities, *Charles Harrison's "preacher play" concerning the affairs of a small town congregation, was a perennial favorite.*

You know, that it's a great gift to have the faculty of making people laugh. It's a great gift to be funny without trying to be funny, just a look, shake of the head or the gesture of the hand, a short, pithy expression, and the multitude goes into a fit of laughter, and the spokesman really wonders what on earth they are laughing about, that's the born humorist, funny and don't know it. That's Harley Sadler, and all of West Texas are wending their way to his tent show to laugh and be glad.

Paul Thardo-Kalmbacher remembers Harley as a "fast, jumping-up-and-down Toby," an energetic, in-motion kind of performer who was always doing something to make the audience laugh, one who would be gasping for air when he came offstage. As age slowed the comedian somewhat, he learned to perform without such reckless expenditure of energy. Flo Darling, who was with the show in the '40s, recalls the Sadler Toby as "...rather meek, sometimes shy, always lovable. This is why it was such a welcome triumph when he outsmarted the villain."

Among Harley's peers, the tent show professionals, opinions varied concerning his acting abilities. If a Top Ten list had ever been compiled from the canvas circuit, Sadler's name would have been present—but perhaps not in first position. Every knowledgeable actor has his favorite candidates for various roles: Toby, G-string, Master of Ceremonies, Candy Spieler, and others. The Texas showman's name is always mentioned in any discussion of these roles, but with little agreement in ranking. Suffice to say that he was well regarded by his fellow players.

Critical pronouncements by the panjandrums of the press are virtually nonexistent. The tent shows were never blessed (or cursed) with much attention from the newspaper reviewers, and except for occasional condescending articles in city papers (informing urban dwellers of the existence of this quaint folk drama) little appeared in print beyond such enthusiastic endorsements as that previously quoted from the *Albany News*.

Undoubtedly the underlying character of the performer was always visible no matter what role was being portrayed. Harley was always Harley, just as John Wayne was always himself in slightly varying permutations. In popular entertainment, transmutability of character is more of a handicap than a virtue; audiences want an always-recognizable commodity, want to know what they're going to see *before* they purchase a ticket.

In common with many professional performers, all the Sadlers, Harley, Billie, and later Gloria, had the ability to project likeableness across the footlights; to be, regardless of role, a person each member of the audience wanted to have as a friend. The story is told of an angry young cowboy who shot out of the buzzard roost one night and was stopped by an usher as he was about to vault up on the stage. "Didn't you hear what that feller said?" he exclaimed angrily, shaking an agitated finger at the villain of the evening. "That so-and-so called Harley a liar!"

In his performance, Sadler tended to avoid overstatement: stagey, actorish flourishes which might call attention to technique. The rest of the company tended to conform to their star's unassuming naturalness. Dramatic performances were expected, but this did not mean scenery-chewing or histrionic trickery. Within the limits of scripts that were not noted for subtlety of characterization, the actors played sincerely and honestly. Bob Siler, a multi-talented actor-musician who was with the show for many years, recalls that in *Seventh Heaven*, a drama about a blind little girl, "I'd get to crying so hard I couldn't get my lines out."

Three or four act plays were presented during the late twenties, with vaudeville at each intermission. Sometime specialty acts like performing dogs were carried with the show, but usually the actors themselves supplied the entr'acte entertainment: standup comedy routines, dramatic monologues, blackout skits, song-and-dance teams, jugglers, ventriloquists, magicians, hillbilly bands, singers, instrumentalists—the list is almost endless. Performing children remained a staple commodity.

These vaudeville turns were as important in pleasing audiences as the plays themselves, and specialty acts were billed as prominently as the play title. (Some successful tent companies used an evening's program of vaudeville—broken by brief ten or fifteen minute scenes from an inconsequential play.) Like most of the spectators interviewed, Louise Hefner Sorensen retains only a hazy memory of the dramas that were presented; but the vaudeville was "incredibly gorgeous." She particularly remembers a specialty dance team, the woman in a black evening gown of the twenties, the man in white tie and tails, as they danced slowly and dreamily to "Three O'Clock in the Morning," with only their faces illuminated by tight follow spots operated from the back of the reserved section. "To me," she says with a remembering smile, "it was very sophisticated." The editor from Albany confirms her

Harley in one of several variations of the clownish Toby.

Harley in makeup and costume for one of his popular "G-String" roles. Billie, his attractive and well-groomed wife, usually avoided being photographed in country attire.

Harley as a bellboy Toby.

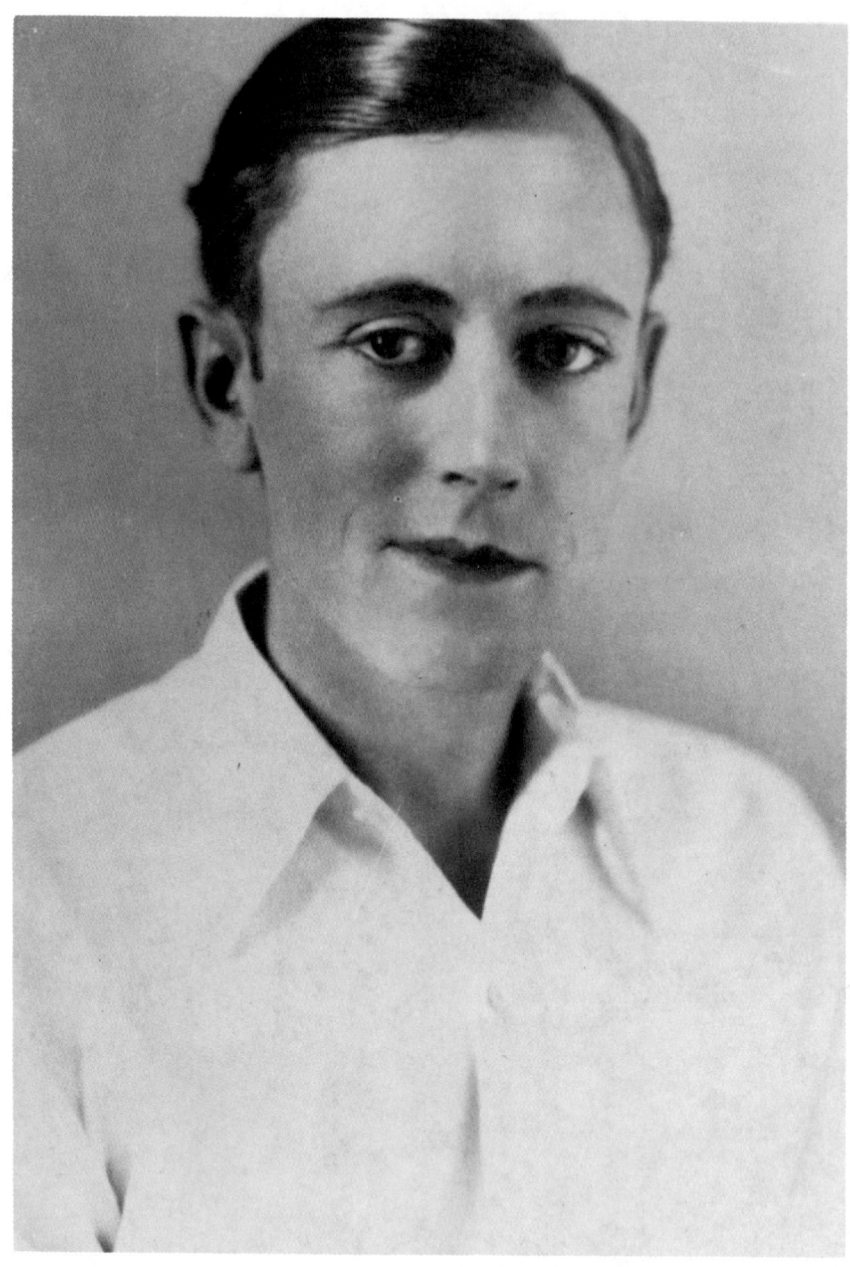

Harley in juvenile makeup. He was probably in his late thirties when this photograph was taken.

favorable opinion: "The vaudeville stunts between the acts were worth the price of the show, each act brought the house down, and think of it not a single vulgar stunt was pulled."

Somewhere between the acts, Harley made the bally candy pitch common to all tent shows. (He avoided a pre-show sale, feeling that people should not be asked to shell out more money after having just paid the price of admission.) Still wearing his show costume, the owner-manager would step around the curtain with a vendor's tray slung around his neck. He frankly admitted, as did most candy pitchmen, that the few pieces of saltwater taffy contained in the boxes of his tray were not particularly valuable nor even very edible. Having gained some audience confidence by pointing out the fault of his product, Harley would motion to the stage. The curtain rose, revealing a stage covered with prizes which ranged from typical carnival stuffed animals, rhinestone jewelry, and stuffed animals, to small but genuine diamond rings. Usually included were such items as rocking chairs, canning kettles, cake dishes, radios, often purchased from local merchants as a means of gaining their good will.

Assuring potential customers that every tenth box contained either a shiny quarter or a coupon good for one of the prizes onstage, Harley and several helpers descended to the audience level, selling boxes of candy about as fast as they could hand them out. While the band played galloping music, people rushed forward to buy five, ten or more boxes at a time. There were shouts and squeals as someone extracted a coupon from a lucky box and ran up on the stage, where a smiling Billie Sadler waited to hand the person a prize. For West Texans, the "bally candy" (from ballyhoo) sale was as exciting as a good horse race. For Sadler, this bit of gambling (forbidden by law, but not enforced in his case) helped build the excitement of the evening—and not incidentally provided him with a very valuable supplement to his income. As with everything else, the candy pitch was handled quickly; nothing could be allowed to interfere with the fast pace of the presentation.

Before the last act of the play, usually after a short vaudeville number, Harley would step in front of the curtain for his talk to the audience. It was more conversation than a speech, since he possessed that ability to establish an almost immediate rapport with an audience. If he happened to be playing a Toby that night, he would remove the tousled red wig, emphasizing that he spoke as himself, not as a stage character. Anyone else would have looked ridiculous, but for Harley this half-madeup condition seemed to add to his natural dignity.

As a necessary part of business, the manager would always plug the show for the following night, telling something of the plot, the actors who were to have featured roles, what vaudeville would be presented. Local events were always publicized, even when they represented competition. He usually had a kind word for his bitterest rival, the motion picture show manager. "This man's doing the best to bring you good, wholesome entertainment," Harley would say, "and you need to patronize him."

Often he would preach a short sermon, a homily about loving, or forgiving, or helping: by the conclusion he would have his audience nodding in agreement as he made his points. Then he would walk to the left side of the curtain, turn, smile shyly, and say the same lines every night: "And so, at the end of the last act, I bid each and every one of you a fond good night." Applause covered his exit.

Members of the orchestra stole silently into place as the final act of the play was winding down to a satisfactory conclusion, so that they were ready to play the "chaser" after the curtain calls were completed. "Good Night Sweetheart" was one of Harley's favorite concluding tunes, but if this were the first of two shows that night (as so often happened on Friday and Saturday) a quick march was used to hurry the departing spectators. The entire show, from overture through play, vaudeville, candy pitch, and curtain speech, was completed in a little over two hours.

On Saturday, "getaway night," a "concert" would often be added after the last performance. Tickets for this program, consisting of an hour of straight vaudeville, would be sold before the last act began, and usually half the audience would remain, everyone moving down to the reserved seat section when the regular performance was concluded.

Tear-down began while the concert was in progress. At the front of the tent, the marquee and ticket office were removed; then bleachers were silently taken apart behind the rapt audience; and finally, vacant chairs would be folded and taken to waiting trucks and wagons. Scenery and costumes were packed away as each act finished, and the concluding number was performed on a totally bare stage. The audience never seemed to mind that the show was vanishing around them. By the end of the concert, a considerable portion was already on its way to the railroad siding where baggage cars were open and waiting.

On weekdays, the actors would be slow to take off their makeup, exchanging views about good and bad points of the evening's performance, discussing changes for the following one. Some of the men hung around the stage, waiting for the beginning of the crap game that could not start until the last of the towners had departed. Gambling was Harley's only apparent vice, and he bet at almost any opportunity: poker, dice, golf and baseball were among his favorites. Not the skillful kind of gambler who won consistently, neither was he the compulsive type who was willing to risk home, livelihood and happiness on a game of chance. When he lost heavily, it was money that he could afford to lose. One eyewitness verifies at least one thousand dollar roll in this backstage game, with Harley making his point, but usually the action was somewhat more restrained.

Rumors of this crap game drifted from the tent to the main streets of these little towns, and may have tarnished Sadler's otherwise spotless reputation. The same saintly hypocrites who eagerly gambled on a dozen boxes of bally candy in hopes of a prize regarded tales of backstage gambling as a subject for much head-shaking and tongue-clucking.

By the time the game began, most of the actors had headed downtown for a late supper, often with local friends. Canvas boss Burnie Massengale or some of his workers stayed with the tent all the night, partly in case of a sudden wind or downpour, partly to see that the town boys were not up to any mischief. Charlie Myers, treasurer for the show, finished counting the night's receipts, often over $500, then stuffed the money into a well-worn canvas satchel with a shoulder strap. He walked, usually alone, back to his room where this small fortune was stuffed beneath his bed until the banks opened the following morning. He never thought of carrying a gun, or of even asking someone to walk with him as he left the tent. He was never robbed.

As the actors entered the restaurants downtown, they would find the walls lined with townspeople who had come to watch them eat. These watchers seldom spoke—even to each other—but they made mental note of every little detail of behavior, every overheard scrap of information. Traveling actors were, in these small towns, the very embodiment of glamor, and their actions were observed as raptly as a later generation was to study the personal habits of movie stars.

The exhilirated performers lingered over their third or fourth cup of coffee; finally, as onlookers slowly faded from their observation posts, a yawning waitress herded them, still laughing and talking, to the cash register and out the front door. By two or three o'clock, the excitement had worn down a little, and the troupe was ready for bed, ready for a night's sleep so that they could begin all over again the following day.

Chapter Five

Success Story: Rag Opera to Riches

THE NINETEEN TWENTIES represent the heyday of the tent show. For Sadler, then at the peak of his career, these were the days of unbelievable prosperity. One newspaperman wrote that the owner/manager was "a taxpayer in more counties than people have fingers." Another journalist, writing in the mid-twenties, described the showman's empire as consisting of "two farms in Crosby County, one in Jones, another in Dawson, a beautiful theatre building in Sweetwater... and his high class stock company." Not mentioned but certainly included in this catalogue of wealth were numerous vacant lots in various downtowns, purchased to ensure a suitable playing location during the show's annual visit, and an interest in several other tent troupes which attempted to capitalize on Harley's reputation by traveling as the "Sadler-Davis" or the "Sadler-Hefner" show.

Two sets of figures remain which give some indication of the financial scope of the operation. The first was published in 1927 by Sadler himself, and seems to have been in response to whispered criticism that he was reaping an inordinate profit from the show's operations. He listed the annual expenses as follows:

Actors and Musicians	$58,000
Common laborers	3,000
Baggage demurrage	550
Telegrams and telephones	225
Misc. and extra labor	2,229
Advance man	1,282
Local drayman	1.500
Occupation taxes	1,028
Donated to civic organizations	7,456.60
Electricity (exclusive of sponsors payments)	1,325.03
Posters,lithos, etc.	3,018.67
Newspaper advertisements	1,350.36

Exterior of the Sadler tent. Location is probably in Austin, based upon lettering on the spare tire cover in the foreground. Latest identifiable car in the 1930 or '31 model.

Repairs, locally bought   2,272.77
Truck payment and expenses   2,325.38

These expenditures, based upon his income tax return for that year, totaled over $85,000, and did not include "a stock engagement which showed a loss of $3,899.60." While not giving his annual income, Sadler did note that "we made less than 15 percent gross profits on our year's business."

Some indication of the weekly income of the show is revealed by three sets of sponsor's records from the village of Slaton, 1927-'29, rescued from the dump by Magnus Klatenhoff, Jr., a dedicated antique car buff who was scavenging for parts. These figures, written in Charlie Myers' careful script, were prepared for the Slaton Volunteer Fire Department, and indicate that this hamlet, population 3,876 in 1930, was a good theatre town—at least for the Sadler aggregation.

In October 1929, Sadler's Comedians played a six-day stand in this West Texas farming community. Their smallest audiences assembled on Wednesday, the traditional church night, when 944 backsliders foresook the temple for the tent.* The second show presented on Saturday night drew the largest house, 1,504, and the week's total attendance was 8,094—more than twice the population of the town.

Gross ticket sales for the six-night run totaled $2,408.60, with income from concessions, bally candy sale, and advertising probably bringing the grand total for the week to more than $3,500. These figures seem insignificant in terms of the present-day value of the dollar, but a look at advertisements in a 1929 newspaper from Lubbock, a few miles from Slaton, gives a truer picture of just how much purchasing power this income represented. Men's shoes were offered for $3.95, "hand-tailored" suits sold for $18.50 up, and a "fine wheat farm near Clovis" could be purchased for $15 an acre. Swift's Cloverleaf bacon was 35¢ a pound, lettuce was 6¢ a head.

The volunteer firemen received ten percent of the ticket sales, or $240.86, from which they paid a light bill of $25 and a lot rental of $30. Apparently no license fee was charged by the town. In answer to a query from Slaton's mayor, a letter explained that the profit was spent on such items as a desk, a

---

*In some towns, the Wednesday evening service was moved up to six o'clock so that congregations could also attend the show.

radio, slickers, hats, boots, socks, and gloves, with the remainder paying the volunteers' "tailor bills, which run at least $9.00 per fire."

Further records reveal that not all tent shows were doing as well as Sadler's. In 1928, a month before the annual arrival of Harley's company, the Merry Madcaps Company appeared in Slaton for only two nights. The Madcaps played to audiences of 276 and 308,had a total income of $253.55, and left the Fire Department with a profit of a little over twenty-five dollars. Expenses for the lot and lights are not shown, but if charged, they would have resulted in a deficit.*

What accounted for Sadler's phenomenal success? In the broadest sense, kinship, a sense of family, seems to have formed the basis. Audiences were like family, and the annual arrival of the troupe in a community was not unlike the homecoming of relatives who had moved to another region.

Harley tended to return to the people who knew him best. In desperate times of drought or depression he might lead his troupe into such foreign lands as East Texas, Kansas, Southern Colorado, and Oklahoma, but forays into unfamiliar territory were not usual. Usually, his range extended no farther east than Galveston beach, where "dead men," huge logs with cable loops attached, were buried deep in the sand to anchor the tent guy ropes. From there, the Sadler kingdom extended northwestward, encompassing such barren areas as that around Wink, where solid rock required the star-drilling of holes before any kind of stake (usually the axle from one of Mr. Ford's model T's or A's) could be put down at all. El Paso marked the western boundary of the realm, extending from there northeasterly across the corner of New Mexico into the Texas Panhandle and such towns as Dalhart, Dumas and Borger.

This territory-wide "family" had its roots in the literal Sadler family which formed the nucleus of his company. Billie, his wife, kept an eye on the bookkeeping and box office, as well as playing the leading lady roles. Gloria, the Sadlers' only child, born in 1922, began working at the

---

*Sadler seems to have been the nemesis of this troupe. In a letter written August 28, 1930, Madcaps' manager Harry Hearn complained to fellow manager Harvey Haverstock that even proximity caused problems: "We were unfortunate enough to play towns near Harley Saddler [sic], and the towns we played were billed for Saddler, this naturally drained us a little as the Elite? of the towns naturally made a trip or two to see his show, and apart from that, considerable passes were given out also."

Sadler's recently motorized street band in San Antonio, around 1930.

family trade as soon as she was able to toddle on stage. Her maternal grandmother, Louise Massengale, joined the show originally to care for the young Gloria, but she quickly became dresser, seamstress, general backstage handy-person. A generation of performers regarded "Mamma Lou" as an indispensible behind-the-scenes helper.

Seth Burnett "Burnie" Massengale, Billie's brother, spent most of his adult life with the show. A large, rawboned man left somewhat retarded by a virulent attack of childhood measles, he worked mainly as a canvasman for his brother-in-law. Many little boys knew him as the shambling giant who dragged them out by the hind leg when they attempted to slip under the tent sidewall.

Ferd, Harley's younger brother, served as advance man on the show, and Gladys, his wife, sold tickets. Their two daughters, Marie and Toby, did specialty routines for the vaudeville during summer vacations, and were usually surrounded by a host of other Sadler nieces and nephews who also worked for their famous uncle.

The troupe represented an extension of the Sadler family. Composed mainly of stable family groups, his actors and workers remained with Sadler for many seasons, becoming as much a part of the clan as if they had been born members. During the good years before the depression, Harley maintained a payroll that was chronically inflated with unneeded employees: he found it much easier to accept people than to disown them.

The prosperous manager served as a caring, considerate, and indulgent father-figure to his troupe. In the years of the twenties, money flooded the Sadler treasury, but it flowed out at the same rate. Salaries were the best paid on any tent show, and Harley's generosity reached almost legendary proportions. Bart Couch, a longtime actor/musician with the show, recalls that a two weeks' stay in a Lubbock hospital with typhoid fever was not only paid for by his manager, but money had been sent him to buy a new topcoat so that he wouldn't get a chill on the trip south to rejoin the troupe. One Christmas, as the company dispersed for the holidays, a lonely Couch was given money for train fare to San Francisco so that he could be reunited with a mother he had not seen for many years.

In the lean years of the depression, money was not as plentiful, but what there was Sadler still dispensed with openhandedness. Couch, who seemed to have lived his improvident juvenile roles offstage as well as on, once saw some of Billie's jewelry go into a pawnshop so that he would have enough money to keep up his payments on a new automobile.

The successful manager's generosity was not confined to members of his company. Several actors remember a daily lineup of unemployed performers behind a San Antonio theater where the company was appearing in a winter stock engagement. Harley, seated onstage, summoned each petitioner to him for a brief conversation. As he listened intently to each account of bad fortune and calamity, he would peel several bills from his omnipresent roll, give the out-of-luck "friend" a pat on the shoulder and turn to hear the next tale of woe.

Harley's largesse was not limited to show people. Gil Lamb, who spent several seasons with the troupe, describes a backstage drama which he witnessed frequently during tours of the chronically drought-stricken Panhandle region. Although he seldom heard more than snatches of the conversation, the action was easy to follow.

Scene: Backstage after a performance. Harley, still wearing costume and stage makeup, leans against a wardrobe trunk, listening intently to a gaunt farmer clad in worn overalls. The farmer's lined face wears a tense, anxious expression, and as he talks, Harley's happy, after-show countenance changes to mirror the other's.

Finally, Harley speaks so that others can hear him: "Charley, would you step over here a minute?"

From behind his desk, the show's treasurer grunts, rises with a noisy sigh, throws a "well, here we go again!" glance at Gil standing in the background, and walks over to the waiting pair. The three engage in earnest conversation; Charley breaks off from the group and walks back to his desk. Taking the cash box from a drawer, he begins to count a pile of bills.

Still talking earnestly, Harley and the farmer walk over to the treasurer's desk Charley hands the money to his boss who in turn hands it to the farmer, whose face now wears an expression of joy mixed with disbelief. Harley puts his hand on the farmer's shoulder, and his voice becomes audible. "Jim Bob, you're going to make a bumper crop next year. I just know it. Now, don't you worry any more."

Charley Myers has been busily scratching a loan agreement on a sheet of paper, but his employer takes the pen from his hand. "Don't bother about that, Charlie: We don't need any paper with old Jim Bob here."

As Jim Bob tries to express his thanks, Harley steers him toward the exit flap in the tent. "Now, don't you worry about a thing; we can settle up when we come through next fall." After a quick handshake, Harley beats a hasty retreat, pausing to call after the departing farmer, "—and say hello to May and the kids for me, will you? That oldest boy still going to make a shortstop?"

Lamb watched this scene, with minor variations, many times during his years with the show. By 1930, according to Myers, the ever-generous manager had over $80,000 in unsecured loans spread among the farmers and ranchers of West Texas and Eastern New Mexico.

By 1929, Sadler's reputation was so established that he could bill his troupe unashamedly as "Harley Sadler and His Own Company—Truly a West Texas Institution." A *Billboard* reporter, visiting the show in that year, wrote:

In towns, large or small no ill word is spoken of Harley Sadler or his company. Everybody boosts him....Harley Sadler knows more people by their first name and is called by his first name by more people than any Governor the State of Texas ever had, in this high, wide, windy West Texas area.

The *El Paso Times* observed that,

This man, not yet 38 years old, is known and loved by thousands and thousands of West Texas folks, because he knows and loves every one of the more than 40 communities in which he lives for a short time each year. Yes, he lives in the towns he plays. He belongs to many of their Chambers of Commerce, and is an active member of the West Texas Chamber of Commerce. He plays golf with them at their country clubs. He helps maintain public activities, and is always on hand to take a personal part in any special work that may be in progress during the week he is in the town. His band and orchestra are at the disposal of the people for school and charitable entertainments, public meetings, football games and similar affairs.

Billboard quoted one official as stating: "We have a town ordinance against tent shows. A clause of it provides for a fine of $50 for every performance presented. However, when Harley Sadler comes to town we forget about the fine. His company is different."

Even with the almost universal adulation that Harley received, and in spite of the fact that tent shows were a generally accepted form of entertainment, there was always some opposition. Rural America had an almost medieval horror of the landless man. To the outlaw litany of "gypsies,

tramps and thieves" named in the popular song of a few
years ago, might very well be added "strolling player."

There was antagonism from the motion picture owner,
who had managed to ally himself with local business
interests in an effort to keep the interlopers from "taking the
money out of town." This argument, one used against the
numerous chain stores which were invading every hamlet,
proved effective, and many citizens refused adamantly to
trade with any but a local merchant. The counter argument,
that the motion picture manager sent most of his admission
fees to Hollywood, fell on deaf ears.

And although the tent show people were diligently
religious, many churches regarded them as outside the
established boundaries of Christianity. So it has always
been since Tertullian, a theologian of the second century,
argued that the sincere Christian foreswore theater when he
was baptized.

Even with his apparent virtues, life was not all cakes
and ale for the prosperous manager. When he moved out of
his regular territory in 1930 to show in Wichita, Kansas, the
movie house owners objected strenuously. According to *Bill
Bruno's Bulletin*, the picture people

Raised their voices in protest at the opposition threatening them and the
city council was . . . begged to pass an ordinance raising the present license
fee of $20 per week to $100 per night . . . . The attorney for the chain made the
plea that it was "unfair to have to compete with concerns which cut into the
summer theatrical trade without leaving any tax money, rentals of
consequence, or profits behind them."

In 1931, when Sadler attempted to repeat a successful
four weeks' engagement in the Texas capitol city of Austin,
the movie owners pointed to an ordinance which forebade a
travelling show to appear more than one month in any year.
The show's local sponsors, fellow Shriners of Sadler's,
appeared before the city council and the law was taken off
the books.

Numerous tax laws were passed in an effort to
discourage the rag opries; there seemed to always be
legislators willing to do the bidding of the movie industry. In
1923, the Baldwin Bill was passed at the third special
session of the Texas Legislature. In the rush to adjourn, few
members of the legislature realized just how harshly
discriminatory the law was. The bill spoke bluntly:

. . . the object and purpose of this act (is) to impose a tax upon such shows,

The Christmas advertisement which appeared in the 1928 Billboard.

amusements and representations as are given by performers traveling from place to place giving exhibitions for private profit other than in regularly established and recognized places of amusement.

....

Provided, however, that nothing in this Act shall be construed to impose a tax upon traveling shows giving exhibitions for private profit in regular established theaters....

To combat such unfair treatment, the tent show managers attempted to form organizations intended to bring some sort of collective action to bear. In 1915, COMA, the Car-Owning Managers' Association, was born, interested to some extent in repressive legislation, but mainly concerned with the ever-increasing transportation rates being charged the touring shows by the railroads. In 1921, Sadler wrote *Billboard* proposing a series of state organizations, since "a lawyer or manager in Texas doesn't know of the exact conditions of proposed laws in Minnesota." His efforts resulted in the creation of the Southwestern Tent Show Managers' Association, and he served as president for its few years of existence. Through his efforts the Baldwin Bill was declared in a test case, "unconstitutional, as the classification is arbitrary and capricious." Since the Association lacked a treasury, Sadler bore most of the legal expenses himself.

Shortly after this, a national organization, the Tent Repertoire Managers' Protective Association (TRMPA) was established, with Paul English, a southern manager, as president and Sadler as vice-president. While never a tightly knit or well-supported organization, TRMPA did serve to promote a certain camaraderie among the scattered tent show fiefdoms. For the two years of its existence, President English's weekly columns in *Billboard* detailed problems being encountered around the country, and the attempts made to combat them, none of which was very successful. In spite of a general acceptance of the tent shows by the rural citizen, persecution by various groups remained a nagging problem.

Taxation was only a part of the harassment. Sadler, in his prosperous days, purchased numerous downtown lots to ensure himself a choice playing location, having been frozen out of suitable sites by past conspiracies. This happened routinely to many tent companies. When Roy E. Fox, in the early twenties, attempted to repeat a successful week's stand in Woodward, Oklahoma, he found that newly created "fire limits" would not permit him a downtown location. According to *Bill Bruno's Bulletin,* Fox secured a lot owned by the Santa Fe Railroad, but the motion picture show manager immediately contacted "the Santa Fe authorities, requesting—nay, commanding—that these intruders be denied the privilege of showing in opposition to the tax-paying citizen." In this case the railroad stood firm and permitted Fox, a good customer, to pitch his tent on their property.

Preachers of fundamentalist persuasion also took a turn at persecution, since play-going was a sin and players were instruments of the devil himself. Concerning the sacrosanct Sadler, their imprecations remained muted, but they never entirely ceased. When the New Harley Sadler Show opened at Texas Tech in the summer of 1976, one of the first persons in the ticket line was an elderly lady who purchased her seat with particular relish. She was, she explained, the daughter of a West Texas minister, and had always been forbidden to set foot in the Sadler tent. Now, she had her first opportunity to find out just what transpired beneath this canvas ceiling. Needless to say, she was not shocked by the proceedings.

No recorded affront to Sadler ever rivalled that received by the Rentfrow Company during the Great War. J.N. Rentfrow, leader of an established and respected troupe, found that he was unable to play the South Texas town of Navasota because a paramilitary organization called the National Council of Defense "did not want tent or traveling shows until after the war, as it took too much money out of town." Rentfrow wrote to one of the national trade journals:

They [the NCD] proceeded to place sentries and station picket guards on all streets leading to the show. The colored population of the city was informed their heads would be knocked off if they came near the show.... We were compelled to close for that week and remain in the city. The next day a committee came to our tent and virtually arrested every male member of the company and took them up to town to find out if they had registration cards and investigate them, trying to find if they were slackers.

A great many other outrages were inflicted upon us, and while our stay in Navasota lasted life was very miserable. The citizens of the town were very much in sympathy with us and declared it an outrage and a disgrace to the city.

While Sadler never experienced such overt hostility, he could not help but be aware of the deep-seated anti-theatre feelings which always lay just beneath the surface of the small towns

A Sadler Christmas card, from the late 20's.

in which he appeared.

But if he remained suspect in his own country, his fame had spread far beyond his playing region—at least among members of the profession. "I've got to meet this Sadler feller," said Chick Boyes, a well-known Nebraska tent show operator. "I want to shake the hand of a manager that hasn't got an enemy in the world."

"Harley Sadler is a good, clean, square-shooting manager, and certainly deserves all the success he seems to be enjoying," wrote Paul English, president of the TRMPA in pages of *Billboard.*

Kelly Masters, sitting in a cold jail cell in Great Falls, Montana, in 1922, had good reasons to remember Sadler's reputation as friend of those in trouble. Master's stock company had gone broke, causing irate creditors to clap the youthful manager behind the bars of the county jail. "STOCK COMPANY OPENS JAIL ENGAGEMENT," headlined the local newspaper. Masters, who was later to become a highly successful writer of children's books under the pen name of Zachary Ball, could think of no one to turn to but a Texas manager whom he had met casually a time or two. He sent a telegram outlining his problems, and received in reply a money order for $150. This was enough to satisfy the first rank of creditors, but not enough to get him out of jail. A second telegram brought another $100, and a third wire still another $100. With the last remittance came the message,

BETTER COME WORK FOR ME

HARLEY

Masters, a much better leading man than manager, did as ordered, spending a season in winter stock with the Texas showman.

Sadler cast a great many loaves on the waterless plains of the Southwest, and while not many were returned with the biblical multiplication, there were some recipients who tried to make repayment with more than words of gratitude. Ferd Sadler recalls a time when he found himself dining for free at a Lubbock restaurant. Years before, it turned out, brother Harley had come across the restaurant owner sitting disconsolately on the running board of his car. The restaurateur's luck had gone sour: he was out of gas, out of money, and several miles from the nearest town. The sandy-haired comedian had taken time to give the unhappy traveler a push to town, then supplied him with money for gas and a little food. More importantly, he had given him hope in the future—and now, the Sadlers dined for free in his cafe.

Chapter Six

"The Little Giant Who Runs the Sunday School Show"

AS COMPANY MANAGER, Sadler sought to maintain a position somewhere between repressive discipline and parental overindulgence. Since his usual response to a problem was more emotional than reasoned, there was nothing that resembled a standard operating procedure. There were, however, some general principles which seem to have governed his operation of the show.

Above all, continuing success was based upon maintaining a presentation which pleased audiences and having a company which exuded an air of moral uprightness. If either of these qualities faltered, his show lost its marketability.

Fast pace and vitality were hallmarks of the Sadler show. "Come on, let's troupe, let's troupe!" Sadler could be heard whispering urgently behind the front curtain when a vaudeville act lingered a little too long in front of the footlights. There must be no halt or hitch in the pace of the performance, no "dead air." Henry Brunk recalls that as a novice curtain puller, he once found himself face to face with a manager demanding to know why the act curtain was late coming down.

"Why, Harley," the startled young man replied, "that actor told me to hold for a couple of seconds after he finished his speech."

"You listen here," replied Harley, shaking a reproving finger under Henry's nose, "that actor isn't running this show—and I am! Now, as soon as he starts his last word, you let go of that rope. And let the pipe bounce on the floor, so it'll start the applause."

A proper moral tone was almost a requirement for the successful show which toured a specific region. Although fly-by-night carnivals might carry rigged games and girlie shows into a community for a few nights, stable troupes

A prosperous manager/owner/star stands outside his tent in the late 20's.

which expected to maintain (and defend) a territory, could not afford to offend the standards of the community in which they played. With Sadler, purity was more than an economic necessity: for him, clean entertainment became almost a crusade. "I don't believe that the people out here care for bedroom farces and sex plays, and they do like a play that has a moral theme running through it," he told an El Paso reporter. "The play was good and is clean," runs a typical review, this one from the *Stamford Leader*. "Clean show. Never heard a vulgar word or saw a vulgar action," remains one of the commonest recollections of the folk who attended Sadler productions.

Purity that would make a modern-day Disney film seem just a little racy was more than a response to the standards of the audience. Sadler practiced the morality which his company displayed. A dedicated non-swearer who was never heard to tell an off-color story—even in the late hours of an all-night, all-male poker game, he insisted that his company adhere to similar standards—at least in public.

All plays and vaudeville skits were carefully screened for swear words, blasphemies and off-color allusions. Most scripts written for the tent shows were well within the bounds of West Texas mores, but they sometimes required the pruning of a word or two. "Dern" or "dang" was automatically substituted for the forbidden expletive, and "hell" was retained only if required by a strong dramatic climax. "I don't know if cuss words would bring any people into my show," Harley said on more than one occasion, "but I sure know a lot of people they'd keep away."

Cleanliness required constant vigilance on the part of the manager to see that actors did not sneak in some of the forbidden vocabulary or vaudeville performers attempt to get an unauthorized laugh with a suggestive wiggle or an eye-rolling leer. The "Polite Vaudeville" particularly tended to grow a little unmannerly if not carefully tended. New acts especially were examined for any violation of the Sadler code, and any transgression was firmly pointed out. "But Harley," a new trouper would protest, "that line gets my biggest laugh! Why in Dallas—"

"This ain't Dallas," Harley would reply. "This is the country, and out here such things *just don't go!* Now, either you take that out, or we'll have to get somebody else to do your act."

After one or two such encounters with their employer, most performers were prepared to accede to his wishes. But the Whitehouse Twins, a popular song-and-dance team with the show for many seasons, waged an unremitting war with Harley over their slightly "blue" material. Waspish, identical twins whose backstage bickerings with each other became an accepted part of the company entertainment, they began to call their unyielding manager "The Little Giant Who Runs the Sunday School Show." Such a description was not terribly far from the truth.

In our present era of sexual frankness, the limits of good taste in the nineteen thirties is difficult to realize. Perhaps the following "daring" routine may serve as an example.

FIRST MAN: *My wife's in everything.*
SECOND MAN: *Everything, you say.*
FIRST MAN: *Everything! The PTA, she's in that. WCTU, Eastern Star, Ladies Aid—*
SECOND MAN: *Just about everything, huh?*
FIRST MAN: *Yes, yesterday, I brought a friend home to show him our new bathtub, and there was my wife: she was in that, too!*

The gasps of the astonished almost drowned out the laughter of the sophisticated. For most of the audience, the suggestion of feminine nudity was not a laughing matter.

Offstage, the troupers were expected to live within the moral boundaries laid out in the plays they performed. They were required to be well mannered and to avoid quarrels, to be sober and honest, to wear spotless, suitable attire on all occasions. Like Shakespeare's fellow actors at the Globe, they were respected citizens who happened to be engaged in the craft of theatre.

Contact with the towners was carefully regulated. Single men of the company were permitted to date local girls so long as their behavior was gentlemanly, but husbands were enjoined to remain around the home fires. Unmarried women were permitted on the show only if they were part of a family group. Once, when it was discovered that a couple on the show lacked the certificate permitting cohabitation, Sadler offered them a choice: they could close with the show that night or they could tie a legal knot. The following day the couple was wed, with their beaming manager serving as best man.

Hiring, the employer's prerogative, was undertaken with great caution, since taking a new person into the company was the rough equivalent of adopting someone into a family. Firing, as might be expected, was like disowning an errant child. Paul Thardo-Kalmbacher, who grew up under Fox and Sadler canvas, recalls having to wait for several years at the conclusion of World War I to rejoin his parents on the Sadler show. Thardo's services as drummer, xylophonist, and baseball player were badly needed by the company, but Harley could not bring himself to discharge the out-of-beat, over-age drummer who had been with him while Paul served in the army. Finally the incumbent decided to quit the road, and the Thardo family was reunited.

Firing was unusual, but disciplining was not. Generally a call-down consisted of little more than a heart-to-heart talk with the manager. On occasion Harley could turn angry. Generally, his temper was restrained, limited to a cold stare and a flatly spoken "Well, if you don't like it you can just get off the show." June Mundee, a veteran of over twenty years with Sadler, recalls once seeing the slighly-built Sadler so enraged that he struck out at one of his actors. The actor may have suffered a loss of dignity, but Harley broke his little finger in delivering the blow. This was an exception, since violence and temper were not usually part of Sadler's management practices. "I've seen Harley really mad three times in my life," reminisced Bart Couch, a Sadler mainstay, "and all of them were at me."

Discipline on the show was maintained also by peer pressure. Sue Kelley, ticket seller and wife of the boss canvasman, found herself on one memorable occasion chastised much more severely by company attitude than she would have been by a forthright call-down from her manager.

The incident began when Harley had arranged a very important poker game with some Waco businessmen during the depths of the depression. The company was in dire financial straits, and the continuation of the season rested upon the outcome of that game. Harley, together with Sue's husband, Claude, and a pokerwise actress of the company were to gamble with the future of the show. Sue and Billie Sadler were told to stay home.

Being found wanting by their husbands was bad enough, but having another woman found worthy to participate was too much to bear. Locating a sympathetic cab driver with a bottle of "good stuff," the two ladies retired to the Sadler apartment, where they proceeded to drink themselves into a pleasanter state of mind. When the game broke up—with Sadler once more solvent—Harley put his wife to bed and Claude half carried Sue back to their apartment.

Sue awoke next morning with a mouth full of cotton and a full appreciation of why Wacoans referred to their local product as "Old Skullbust." Dismally, she remembered a speech that Harley had made to the assembled troupe only the week before: "The next person who is publicly intoxicated may regard his two weeks' notice as beginning on that date."

For the next two weeks, no one, including her husband, spoke to the contrite Mrs. Kelley of her transgressions, but the absence of any comment about the poker game revealed to her that the incident was known throughout the company. The silence on the subject was deafening, and convinced the offender that her fate was sealed. At the end of the two-weeks' notice period, she approached treasurer Charley Myers for her final salary. "Well, Charley," she said with an attempt at a brave smile, "I guess this is it."

Myers carefully counted out her wages, stacking coins on top of the bills. "You know this show couldn't go on without Billie and your husband," he said, pushing the money toward her, "but I hope you realize what an embarrassment you've caused Harley."

She did, and resolved never to repeat the offense.

There was a great deal of pride felt by members of the company, a feeling enhanced by the knowledge that the Sadler aggregation was regarded as the pinnacle of the tent show industry throughout the nation. Salaries were the highest in the industry, and appreciative audiences gave the performers needed artistic satisfaction. Hard work was rewarded: company members were paid according to the number of assignments they fulfilled. Although usually hired for some special talent, one person might become any combination of actor, musician, vaudeville performer, ticket catcher, candy seller or canvasman. Certain patronage plums, such as the candy and banner concessions, were given to the most industrious, most dependable people.

Harley's people seemed very content with what they were doing. These were not hungry, success-driven performers eager to claw their way to stardom. Many very competent actors found themselves content to work steadily in a pleasant environment before a receptive audience. They avoided the fiercely competitive struggle of Broadway or Hollywood, the endless months of lethargic non-acting interspersed with frenetic bursts of creative activity. With an established tent show, an actor could work at his craft

Mundee and June, a juggling team, began with Sadler as young performers...

...and stayed to become old ones.

steadily without experiencing the tensions, anxieties and insecurities of the Big Time. A competent performer need not worry about wearing out his welcome with his audiences. In popular entertainment, familiarity breeds not contempt but recognition, acceptance and friendship.

With few exceptions, troupers were not college or academy trained. Many had been born into the profession. Others, like Harley, were small town people who all their lives had harbored dreams of going on the stage. Numerous village girls, Billie for one, began their stage career by falling in love with an actor. The auxiliaries, drivers, canvasmen, stagehands, were invariably small town boys entranced by the glamor of show business. They were able to bask in the reflected glory of the performances they helped create.

Specialties counted more than acting abilities when it came to employability. A would-be actor in a small town was wise to spend his time studying music, dancing or acrobatics. Actor training could be acquired on the stage after the performer had been hired for some other talent. Bob Siler, who played leading roles on the Sadler show, was hired originally as a musician. Bart Couch, remembered for his juvenile portrayals, started as a trombonist and progressed to vocalist. Al Pitcaithley, a well-known leading man— although never with the Sadler aggregation—started as a contortionist. Harley himself first left home not because of his acting abilities, but because he could play the trombone.

Very few tent-trained actors ever achieved greater fame than that accorded by their regional audiences. A certain number of them did migrate to Hollywood in the early days of film-making, becoming third-rank players who appeared almost continuously in the pot-boilers of the silent days. Most of them remained recognizable but nameless. There were a handful who did become genuine stars. Will Geer, Lyle Talbot, Milburn Stone, and Charles Winninger all received their early training under canvas.

Harley told many times the story of how, in the early 1920s, he had fired Clark Gable from a winter stock company he was running in Houston. Gable, a handsome, likeable young man, could not conquer the stage fright that seized him when he faced an audience. Rehearsals went smoothly enough, but performances for him were a nightmare: his jaw became rigid, he forgot his lines, cold sweat beaded his forehead. Sadly, the manager let him go, convinced that he would never make an actor. "I fired a million dollars,"

Harley used to say with wry humor in later years.

Chill Wills has claimed for many years that his acting career began with the Sadler company. During the forties Wills was a friend of Sadler's (who was not?) and boasted to the press of his tent show background, an assertion that Harley never denied. No evidence to support this claim has been uncovered, and letters to Wills have gone unanswered.

Jennifer Jones was the only female star of some magnitude associated with Sadler's company, and here some evidence exists to document the association. Several books and numerous Sunday supplement articles have noted this "fact," but all use for verification a photograph showing a large truck parked near a large tent. On the side of the truck is emblazoned:

JENNIFER JONES
with

THE HARLEY SADLER SHOW

The photo proclaims an event which never happened.

Phil Isley, Miss Jones' father, owned a large chain of Southwestern motion picture theatres. He arranged for his beautiful daughter, nee Phyllis Isley, to have a try at Hollywood stardom. The publicity department at Twentieth Century Fox determined that the young Miss Isley needed not only a new name, but also a more romantic background. Her father, a shrewd and knowledgeable businessman of considerable wealth, became, through the magic of publicity, the owner-manager of a small, peregrinating tent show. Jennifer, his renamed daughter, now had a background of growing up as a backstage child with her daddy's fictitious troupe.

According to Isley, the newly-christened Miss Jones did actually spend a few weeks one summer under canvas with the Kansas-based Sport North show to gain some needed acting experience—of which she had little. But even though the Isleys and the Sadlers were good friends, the beautiful young Jennifer never appeared under Sadler canvas. The fictitious billing came about when Harley, joining in the publicity hype, allowed "JENNIFER JONES with" to appear above his show title, granting the headliner position to Miss Jones only long enough for the photograph to be taken. Magnified, the picture shows clearly that, while "THE HARLEY SADLER SHOW" is painted in the spaces between the vertical framing members of the truck body, the temporary billing of the supposed star is done in crisp, new cutout letters that are tacked precariously onto raised verticals.

This photograph proclaims an event that never happened. Miss Jones' fictitious billing occurred during the late 30's or early 40's.

Such machinations, did, for the most part, lie outside Harley's normal pattern of operations. He was not inclined to dabble in affairs that were not part of his immediate domain. Being the ruler of his own little kingdom was sufficient.

Although he had plenty of help in his administration of company affairs, surprisingy little came from Billie, his wife. She preferred to tread a neutral path somewhere between management and labor. Under the circumstances, any other course would have caused jealousy, dissension, and polarization. "She was a fine old gal," said Gil Lamb in an accurate summary, "never acted like a manager's wife, never tattled to Harley. She was just one of the people on the show—who happened to be married to the boss."

The senior Thardo-Kalmbacher, known respectfully as "Mr. Ed.," or "Dad," gave a hand with personnel problems, keeping minor disputes that arose within the company from coming to the manager's attention. By lending a sympathetic ear to members of the troupe, he was able to prevent petty tensions and bickerings from turning into major arguments.

Claude Kelley, the boss canvasman who kept Harley's huge tents aloft in all kinds of Texas weather, kept the sometimes rowdy crews in line, relieving Harley of that responsibility. A big, bluff, blue-eyed Irishman who was later to become sheriff of Kent County, he kept a tight rein on the laboring force, taking care to avoid friction which frquently arises between cast and crew.

Kelley's wife, Sue, worked as ticket-seller, but she also functioned as confidante, advisor, and out-front "eyes" for her manager, reporting frankly on how the show looked from the audience viewpoint.

Although no formal lines of authority were ever established, everyone knew pretty well where his responsibility began and ended. However, within the firm friendships established between people who had spent years together on the show, giving orders sometimes called for extreme tact, as the following story will illustrate.

Ethel Snow was a very popular actress who had been with Harley ever since he first opened as Brunks' No. 3 company. Miss Snow, the wife of business manager Charley Myers, also did a crowd-pleasing vocal as part of the vaudeville. She decided, apparently on her own, to add a dance routine to her act—even though approaching middle age had added more pounds than would agreeably fit into a dancer's abbreviated costume. Sensing that the act was not going over, Harley asked Sue Kelley for an evaluation.

"Harley, when she dances she almost gets boos," Sadler's "eyes" reported ruefully about her good friend, Ethel.

Pensively, the manager paused to digest the information. "Well, Sue." he replied, "I guess you'd better talk to her about it."

"No, sir!" responded Sue, shaking her head, "That's *your* job."

Discussion revealed that neither one of them had the courage to broach the subject. Finally, Harley decided to approach Ethel's husband, Charley Myers. He agreed to talk to her about the problem, and shortly thereafter, Miss Snow's terpsichorean efforts faded from the bill. No one's feelings were ruffled more than was absolutely necessary to maintain the quality of the show.

Charley Myers carried one of the most difficult loads of responsibility: he was required to maintain solvency in spite of the overgenerous nature of his employer. He doubled in brass, playing baritone in the street band, but most of his efforts went toward maintaining some degree of order in the financial affairs of the company. His portable desk with its myriad cubbyholes, a mechanical marvel which folded into a compact box for touring, occupied a prominent position at Stage Right on the ground level. This desk was very familiar to all the company, for it was here that they came to draw their weekly wages. And here the improvident came to try to wheedle an advance on their already over-advanced salaries.

Inevitably Myers became the villain for those who continually existed on money yet to be earned. One actor recalls the business manager as a gruff, Scrooge-like individual who spent all his waking hours poring over the columns in his account books. This same actor, one of the chronically overdrawn ones, remembers particularly one beautiful autumn evening when Ethel Snow stood at the sidewall of the tent, gazing out at the newly-risen full moon.

"Charley," she called, "just come over here and look at this moon."

Laying down his pen, the treasurer pushed his chair away from the desk and shambled over to his wife. Peering at the moon for a long moment he turned to Ethel with a puzzled expression, "What the hell's the matter with it?" he enquired.

Others retain an entirely different impression of this keeper of the purse. Those who worked for him regarded Charley as warm, friendly, and considerate. He was a favorite with the children on the show, and one drawer of his desk was always stuffed with candy and chewing gum.

During the good years when he had a large company, Harley found himself surrounded by people who willingly shared the weight of his responsiblity. Although affairs ran smoothly for the most part, there were two chronic, nagging problems for which solutions were never found: divorce and drinking.

The breakup of apparently stable marriages seemed a part of the nomadic life of the tent show. Perhaps the rootless kind of existence, perhaps the absence of privacy in this hive-like environment, perhaps an excess of togetherness— at any rate, circumstances placed unbearable pressures on partnerships that, under different circumstances, might have survived.

As a result, divorce was an accepted part of life on the tent show during the twenties and thirties, when still a rarity among the populace. Breakups and the occasional triangle were doubly unpleasant for people living together so intimately, since choosing sides became almost unavoidable. Harley, as manager, found there was little he could do beyond listening sympathetically to both sides of the argument, then offering sound advice he knew would seldom be followed. The company heaved a collective sigh when the situation finally resolved itself.

Drinking is a persistent aggravation that has perplexed show managers for centuries. Actors tend to be a convivial lot, and the cry of "Hey, come have a drink," is hard to resist, even if heard an hour before a performance rather than an hour after. In terms of percentage, there were few problem drinkers on the tent shows, but even one inebriated actor can ruin an evening's performance—or so it seems to the sober people who happen to be onstage with him.

The great days of the tent shows were also the times when violating prohibition laws had become almost a national occupation. This was the era of bathtub gin, the hip flask, speakeasy, and straight-off-the-boat concoction supplied (and usually manufactured) by the local bootlegger. Many physicians made a comfortable living by taking up residence in the back of a drug store and dispensing prescriptions for pints of legal whiskey clearly labeled "FOR MEDICAL PURPOSES ONLY." Small town Railway

Express depots had a shelf of parcels addressed to John Doe, and any John (or Jane) with a thirst could pick up a bottle by paying the COD charges. A standard tent show gag had the master of ceremonies reading a message handed him across the footlights: "Will the Reverend Jones please hurry down to the freight office and pick up his crate of hymn books? They are leaking all over the floor."

Sadler was widely regarded as a total abstainer, but in truth he seemed to have no objection to moderate drinking, and would occasionally drink a short beer as if to demonstrate his tolerance. He was, however, almost maniacal in his pursuit of the drinking actor. According to several members of his troupe, he could be standing in the Downstage Right wing and catch the odor of moonshine on the breath of an actor waiting for his entrance Up Left. Ferd, his brother, put it succinctly: "Harley had a nose like a bloodhound."

Ferd remembers one particular evening in Hamlin, Texas, when he was lounging outside the tent, waiting to catch tickets at the front door. The town marshal, beckoning from inside the still-empty tent, handed this youngest of the Sadler brothers a Mason jar half-filled with a colorless liquid. Not wanting to appear a green country boy, Ferd took a mighty gulp: the raw liquor burned all the way down, leaving him half-sick. Wheezing his thanks, he went back to the front of the tent, just in time to see the band parade by. Harley's head swiveled abruptly as he marched by his brother, but nothing was said.

Later that night, after the show, the company was eating at a nearby cafe. Ferd was seated with several people when Harley came in with his wife. Billie found a vacant chair near the door as Harley marched over to where his brother sat.

"Ferd," he said, pointing an accusatory finger, "you were drinking before the show."

Ferd quailed before the anger of his idolized brother. He tried to shift responsibility. "But, Harley," he quavered, "It was give me by the town marshal!"

The appeal to higher authority was lost on the manager. "Brother," he replied, "if you ever do that again, I'm going to have to send you home." As Harley moved across the room to rejoin his wife, Ferd embarked upon a life of total abstinence.

Gil Lamb, an actor-trumpeter-singer on the show for several seasons during the mid-thirties, is a man who plumbed the depths of many a bottle. Today, he is a leading citizen of Muleshoe, Texas, the owner-manager of radio station KMUL. It is hard to conjure up the image of the young hell-raiser whom Harley finally had to run off the show. "I don't remember most of what people say I did in those days," Lamb said in a recent interview, "but they're probably all true.

Gil was not the only drinking actor on the show, but he was one of the few who could not quit in time to sober up for a performance. Matters came to a head during a long run in Austin, the state capitol. The show was very popular there, drawing a mixed audience of students, professors, legislators and townspeople. The usual run was for at least a full month, playing at their standard location of Sixteenth and Guadaloupe, midway between the University of Texas and the Capitol. The long stay caused problems; once the show had settled in, there was little for the actor to occupy himself with during the day. If he had a tendency to drink, the long days of inaction provided an almost irresistible temptation.

"Sheep," as Lamb was known to the company, had received several call-downs about his drinking before and during the show, so no one was particularly surprised to see his place at the makeup table sitting vacant one evening. Harley waited until half-hour was called; he hastily removed his half-finished makeup and left the tent to walk to Lamb's nearby boarding house.

A knock on the actor's door brought no response. "Sheep?" Harley called, "It's getting on toward show time." An answer came from the bathroom across the hall.

"I'm taking a bath, Harley," Gil sang out. "Be with you in just a minute."

"Sheep, you'd better be hurrying up. Can I help—." Here Harley opened the bathroom door and found his performer sitting fully clothed in an overflowing tub. Lamb was retrieved from the bath and dried out—externally, at least. A quart of black coffee and a dash to the tent left the actor in a condition that he could be carried through the show by an understanding but edgy cast.

After the show, the manager sat with his now-repentant Lamb. "Sheep," Harley began, "I love you like a brother, but I don't understand why you do these things.... I'm going to have to let you go." Lamb contemplated the crushed grass beneath his chair as Harley stood up. "I'll buy you a train ticket to anywhere in Texas, and give you a little money to start out on." Vaulting onto the band platform, Sadler turned back: "Oh, the money you owe me for wardrobe, just forget it." He exited through the curtained doorway, leaving a disconsolate Lamb sitting among the vacant chairs.

This was not to be the end of the story. Some time during the early morning, a drunken Lamb stumbled into the tent and fell into a sodden sleep on a crewman's cot. "Sheep's back," someone told Harley.

The slight manager, about half Lamb's impressive size, walked over to the cot and shook him. Lamb, not fully awake, lashed out with a large hand. "Get the hell away from here," he shouted.

Harley easily dodged the flailing hand and struck back, landing a punch on the actor's cheek. He was wearing a diamond ring which left a long, bloody scratch. Lamb put his hand to his face, then looked at the bright blood on his palm. Even drunk, he could easily have broken Sadler like a match: instead he dissolved into tears. "Harley," he said brokenly, "you hit me!"

"I know it, Sheep," Harley replied softly, "—but you made me so *Dee* mad, I couldn't help it." (*Dee*" was as close as he ever came to actual profanity, and that was reserved for moments of great stress.) Helping the now-repentant performer to his feet, he took a silk handkerchief from his breast pocket and dabbed at the blood on Lamb's cheek. "I'm sorry I hit you," he said.

"I know you are, Harley," Lamb replied.

Ferd Sadler had been a witness to the fight: Harley motioned him over. "Brother, we're going over to Sheep's room and help him pack." They drove silently to the boarding house and proceeded to fold and pack the clothing for which Harley had paid. Putting suitcases in the back seat and tying the wardrobe trunk on the rear luggage carrier, Ferd and Sheep got in the front seat. Harley peeled several bills from his roll and handed them to Ferd. "Buy him a ticket to wherever he wants to go in Texas, and just before he leaves, give him these two weeks' wages," Harley instructed.

They drove off. Lamb watched the receding figure until they turned a corner, then settled back in his seat. "Ferd," he said, "I really love that little feller."

Rules about drinking were perhaps the most rigidly enforced of any restrictions on the Sadler show. The rag opries in general exhibited a relaxed attitude toward discipline, sometimes to the detriment of the performance. On many shows the backstage areas were so crowded with friends and visiting performers that the actors had difficulty getting on and off the stage. Sometimes an onstage actor would sidle toward the wings and carry on a whispered conversation with an offstage acquaintance while waiting for his next line.

Harley's behind-the-curtain operation was not that casual. Visitors were permitted backstage, but when half-hour was called, they were politely but firmly ushered to seats out front. The atmosphere in the wings was a blend of efficiency and casualness; businesslike but never solemn. Harley and Marv Landrum had for years maintained an offstage checker game, each making a move when he came offstage. Routinely they accused each other of rearranging the pieces; the whispered arguments reached such heights of mock intensity that newcomers frequently thought that the two old friends were on the verge of blows.

Onstage performances also maintained a casualness about them. Sadler, a master of improvisation, believed that a certain amount of kidding around kept his actors on their toes, relieved the boredom of endless rote performances. "Break-up," that stage game which has delighted audiences for centuries, was played rather often during the lighter moments of a play. Spectators relished seeing the stricken expression of an actor who has suddenly "gone up" in his lines; they joined in laughter as a novice was reduced by an unexpected ad-lib to sputtering, giggling helplessness. "Better watch out or I'll tell Gladys," Harley whispered to Gil Lamb as he exited, leaving the dumbstruck actor standing in the middle of the stage, wondering how Harley had learned about his current romance.

Duels frequently developed in the break-up game. A.C. Hefner and his manager fought unrelentingly, and occasionally one would win. Flo Darling was a cool, controlled actress who never lost a game; when Harley played a scene with crossed eyes, she crossed her own and went on with the scene. Marv Landrum also never lost a game—onstage, at least; but as soon as he exited the stage, he would collapse into a chair, shaking with spasms of silent laughter.

In terms of the present day, actors were woefully under-rehearsed and far from perfect in their lines, a condition which led to a casual regard for the words of the playwright. Typically the show rehearsed for a total of one week before opening a bill of six plays—plus vaudeville. As diligently as actors worked on their parts, there was simply no time to learn them exactly. This led to a semi-commedia style of playing in which the cast followed the general direction of the plot without knowing the exact lines.

Conduct of the rehearsals was left to a "director" who had little time to do more than keep track of entrances and exits, plus rounding up the necessary properties for each scene. He worked usually without the presence of his star, since Harley also served as manager, owner, producer, and head of public relations. The cast knew full well that they would be expected to carry their employer through scenes he would never learn. Many actors tend to be rote learners, and a scene once learned incorrectly will never be "unlearned." Wherever Harley stumbled and improvised in initial rehearsals and performances, he would continue to stumble and improvise for the entire season. "How am I doing?" he once whispered to Bart Couch as he floundered through the middle of the second act.

"About as well as could be expected," Couch whispered back—and walked off the stage!

Harley's jaw dropped. "You little so-and-so! Now, you get back out here and finish this scene!" A grinning Couch strolled back onstage, as the audience hooted.

Frequently, ad-libs and improvisations were better than the lines of the original script, and were incorporated into the play. For examples:

BART COUCH: *(As city slicker leaves farmhouse)* He won't be back soon.

HARLEY: Why is that?

BART: I put a skunk in his suitcase.

****

DAUGHTER: Father, whatever are we going to do?

FATHER: *(Harley, who had never learned the speech which ended the act)*

Do? Why, you can...you can.... Let me see.....

(Slaps mosquito hovering around the warmth of the footlights)

Why, you can bring me the Flit gun! (Curtain)

****

HARLEY *(Answering the phone, but never remembering what the call was about)*

Hello, Sam!....Sam, is that right? .....You don't say so, Sam....Well, Sam, I'll see you tomorrow....So long, Sam.... *(Turns to waiting actors)* You know who that was? That was Sam.

There was a good deal of clowning around among the good-humored members of the company. Once, when Harley

Many tent shows fielded their own baseball teams, playing the local champions on Saturday afternoon. Manager Sadler is pictured at right.

returned to the company after a two weeks' stay in the
hospital to have his appendix removed, he went to the
dressing room and began to don his Toby costume—which
had been worn in his absence by Howard Hack, the only
man of the company small enough to fit into Harley's
clothing. "Howard, don't you ever wash your feet?" enquired
Harley, wrinkling his nose.

Hack, an old friend of Sadler's from showboat days,
looked up in surprise. "I wash my feet all the time," he
replied defensively.

"Yeah? Well, just take a whiff of these boots!" Howard
smelled and gasped. The boots made the round of the
dressing room, each man commenting on the ripeness of Mr.
Hack's lower extremities. Eventually, and before Howard's
feelings could become too ruffled, someone confessed that
Burnie Massengale had dabbed a little limburger cheese in
the toe of each boot.

The orchestra came in for its share of kidding. Actors
recall blowing sneezing powder through the curtained
doorway just as the musicians were beginning their
overture. On another occasion, some wag dropped nails into
the mouthpieces of the brass instruments, rendering them
totally mute. The orchestra was not without means of
retaliation: who can forget the stricken expression on the
face of the smart-alec tap dancer as he realized that the
musical tempo was slowly but inexorably gaining speed
through his number?

Ad-libbing and clowning around did not mean license
on the stage. Woe betide the young actor who thought he
could embroider a small part with some added lines or
snappy bits of business. Such privileges were reserved for
Harley and a few of the older players who were careful not to
abuse their freedom. Actors tend to remember the unusual
more than hundreds of perfectly routine performances, so
that retrospectively these foolings loom out of proportion to
what actually took place.

For the most part the Little Giant ruled very happily
over his group of Sunday scholars, most of whom seemed
very content with their lot in life. Harley found himself
satisfied with what he was doing. Reports of offers from
Hollywood and Broadway surfaced periodically in the
newspapers, but if they were at all serious, Harley never
seemed to have taken them so. Perhaps his youthful failure
in Chicago many years before had soured him on the Big
Time. He preferred, he told interviewers, to stay where he
could "make more money and be his own boss."

Chapter Seven

Change of Fortune: The Depression

PROSPERITY AND POPULARITY had always attended Sadler's managerial career, and he had every reason to feel satisfied with the state of his affairs. In 1929, shortly before the Wall Street Crash, he told an El Paso reporter:

I feel that I have enjoyed and got more out of life than I have been entitled to, more than I have a right to expect. I want to be appreciative of this fact and give back to the people who have helped me all that I can. No doubt there are other shows that have made more money for their owners than mine does for me, but I don't consider profit in dollars all there is to success. A big part of what I call success is the fact that I please the people who are my friends, and give them happy hours and wholesome laughter.

Billy Neff, a former rep actor turned vaudevillian, vouched for Sadler's prosperity. Writing in *Billboard* at the end of '29, he marveled at the Christmas-week show he saw in San Angelo. "How Sadler can give the Texas folk so much show at popular prices is beyond me," he wrote. Neff was invited to join the company for its annual Christmas banquet at the San Angelo hotel, and he remarked that "the good fellowship took me back to the good old days."

Good fellowship may have survived, but the prosperity came to abrupt termination. By 1930 the nation was in the grip of The Depression, and people were more concerned about money for food and clothing than with such luxuries as entertainment. Neil Schaffner, a well-known Iowa tent show operator, recalled that his audiences vanished precisely on July 6, 1930, and that other shows in his area suffered a similar fate on the same date. About that time, the Dubinsky Brothers, operators of the largest tent show organization in the nation, folded eleven of their tents, leaving them with only two on the road. Rolland Haverstock remembers his father, Harvey, standing in front of a near-empty family tent and telling the assembled crowd, "Come on in, neighbors, and see the show!"

"Harve, we'd love to see your show," a weathered farmer

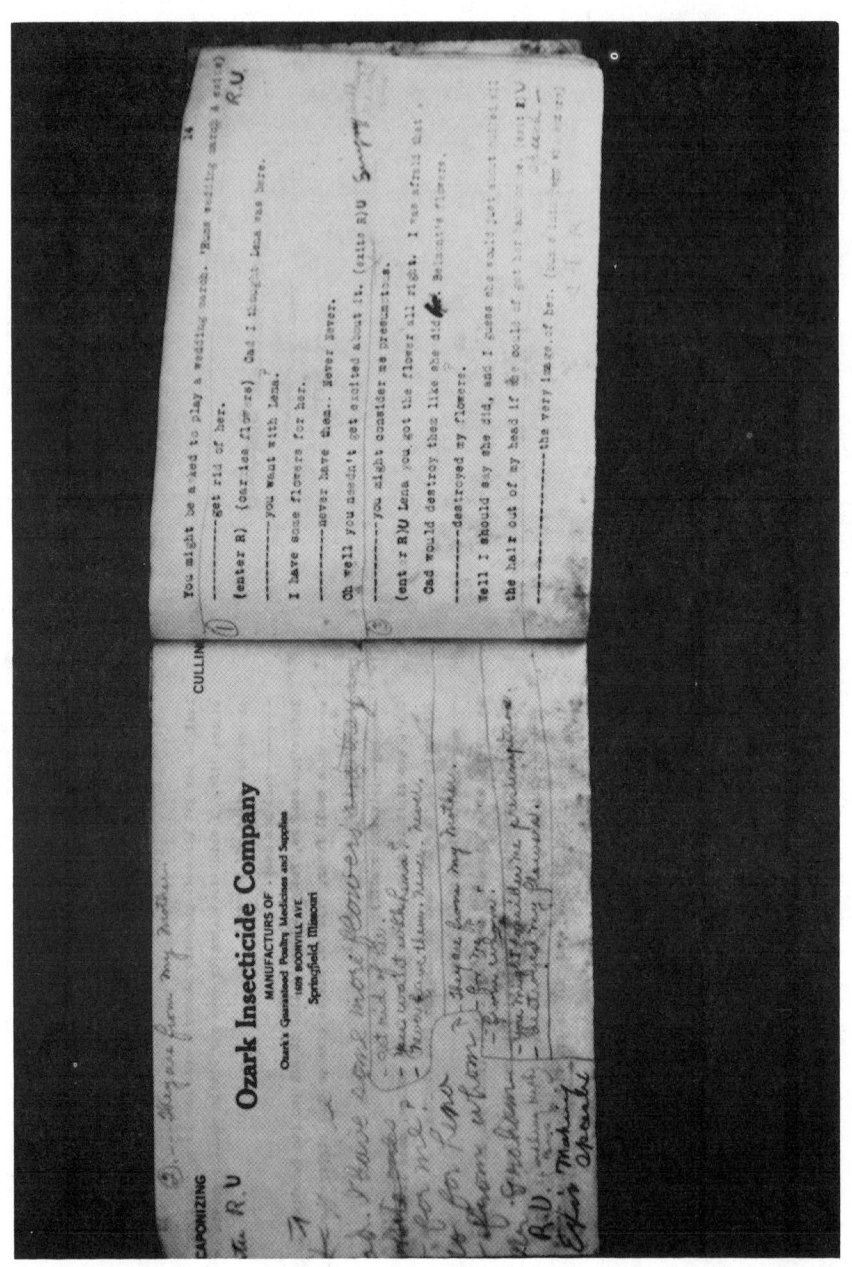

Scripts were seldom published. Actors' parts were copied on whatever paper came to mind.

replied, "but the truth is, we ain't got any money."

"Well, neither have we," replied the elder Haverstock, "so just come on in and enjoy the show. Pay what you can, or don't pay at all if you can't."

For many of the smaller shows like the Haverstocks, a barter system of payment sprang up. Country folk, unwilling to accept charity, began bringing eggs, chickens, garden produce to pay for their evening's entertainment. Mutual poverty provided an even greater bond between the players and their public.

With the depression came an unusual assignment for the Texas manager: having already served as vice president of the *manager's* protective association, he was now elected fourth vice president of the Equity, the *actor's* labor union. His special province was to be the overseer of performers working under canvas.

Putting an owner/manager on the executive board of a labor organization seems at first glance the equivalent to locking the fox in the hen house. However, the division between management and labor was not as sharply defined in the tent show as in other parts of the entertainment industry. Employers and employees worked side by side, sharing good and bad fortune. There was a camaraderie which ran counter to the principles of class warfare.

Actors, always an exploited class of people, had desperately needed a union, but they were slow to organize, lagging a decade or two behind the musicians and stagehands. In the nineteen twenties, many featured performers appearing on the road earned less than the scene shifters and pit musicians who supported them. Exploitation and inadequate wages led many tent show performers to join Equity, so that by the mid-twenties, the Kansas City office of the union, located at the hiring center for the tent shows, became the third largest local in the nation, exceeded only by New York and Chicago.

Policing the tent shows, arriving at some orderly process of bargaining and negotiation, proved almost impossible. Given the transitory, even ephemeral, nature of the rag opries, their lack of centralization, and independence of each little canvas empire, they were really not organizable. Unscrupulous managers still absconded with box office receipts, leaving their employees stranded in Hicksville without money to pay hotel bills. Disloyal actors continued to walk out on contracts when a better offer came their way. By 1930 complaints were piling up from both managers and actors, but union representatives found it nearly impossible to keep track of the peregrinating participants. The desks of the union were piled high with unresolved disputes.

The high water mark for tent show membership in Equity was reached in 1930. Undoubtedly the creation of a special vice presidency to serve their needs was an attempt to placate this constituency at a time when the union's major efforts were concentrated on the much more lucrative film industry. Perhaps Sadler was nominated not only for his popularity but also because it was felt he would not create problems within the union. The editor of *Bill Bruno's Bulletin* thought so. He wrote,

We give Harley Sadler credit for unfailing fairness in the past—no manager's slate is cleaner than his....

We suggest that in the coming election folks vote against Harley Sadler and allow him to remain the splendid manager he now is. Show business needs him as a manager and not as a powerless fourth vice president of Equity to be made the scapegoat for New York.

In office, the "splendid manager" either found himself powerless or did not choose to exert much force on the conduct of union affairs. He had never been a militant, preferring to operate by accommodation and conciliation rather than confrontation. Moreover, as an employer as well as an actor, he was inclined to look at union policy from a divided viewpoint. "Equity works much better for management than it does for the actor," he once confided to fellow manager Henry Brunk.

But whatever Sadler's abilities and shortcomings as a union executive, he was engaged in a losing game. The tent shows were losing popularity, audiences had little money for entertainment, and for every job available in the shrunken companies, there were literally hundreds of actors willing to work under any conditions just for the opportunity to perform. By the mid-thirties, Actors' Equity had faded from the tent show scene.

Sadler's show, with its huge base of popularity and a history of financial soundness, survived the early stages of the depression much better than most. However, by the fall of 1931 *Billboard* reported that the first showman of the Southwest was encountering "tough sledding."

Harley has managed to survive the ordeals of the unusually "tough" summer and meet the weekly payroll regularly. "However, the season was anything but a pipe," Sadler says. "We found the going rough in spots and several of the weeks could be charged up as distinct bloomers. Still I have managed to keep going and make a little money, so I have no right to register a kick."

Many shows were searching for gimmicks which would promote sales at the box office: merchant sponsorships like those used by the chautauquas; ladies' night; twofers; thinly disguised lotteries called by some euphemism such as the "country store"; and, of course, S—E—X! Desperate companies were increasingly leaning to the use of such titles as *What Every Daughter Should Learn, Why Girls Walk Home,* and *Confessions of a Wife* to stimulate business. Harley was never adept at promotion schemes, and he would never consider the use of off-color titles—even if they delivered little of the naughtiness they hinted at.

Sadler was never a very shrewd businessman. Henry Brunk, his good friend for many, many years, regarded him as "a far better actor than manager." In the lean years of the thirties, according to Henry, the ever-generous Sadler "gave out too many comps and kept too large a payroll." Prudence dictated that the successful operator trim his cast, cut out all frills, reduce the size of his operation.

Harley took the opposite tack, enlarging his show to mammoth proportions. He purchased a new tent, one measuring one hundred by one hundred-eighty feet, with a proscenium forty feet wide. Scenery grew to twelve feet in height, rather than the usual eight. According to *Billboard* of September 5, 1931,

Sadler's new tent theater is larger and more beautiful than ever, and that's saying something. The blue and gold color scheme effect is used throughout. This was adopted by Sadler some five years ago.

More than 1,600 chairs are used in the auditorium proper plus the usual bleachers. All seats are covered with heavy orange colored duck, with the exception of 500 leather cushioned, used as numbered chairs for downtown ticket sale.

The huge tent (many felt it could not survive the winds of Tornado Alley) drew a then-record attendance of 2,500 for one performance, in Austin. But the larger outfit had limitations; no longer could Sadler play those many crossroad communities which had been his mainstay. He appeared now in cities such as Waco, Galveston, San Antonio, Fort Worth, and Austin with increasing frequency, needing larger populations to draw upon. And the expense of moving made even a week's stand no longer profitable. He needed to remain at least a month in each location to make money.

And the tent shows were rapidly losing their audience to the now-talking motion pictures ("Squawkies," *Bruno's Bulletin* called them). Not only were these a little cheaper than the tented attractions, but they were better able to satisfy the longings, the appetites, and the desires of their impoverished audience. Seated alone in the darkened theatre, the depressed, the discouraged, the hungry could dwell for a moment in the land of the affluent, the dream world where everyone dressed for dinner, drove new cars, lived in big houses with a legion of servants. The tent show could not offer escape of this magnitude.

Disaster seemed to dog Harley's footsteps during the thirties. A car ran into the truck carrying his street band in 1931, putting several musicians in a Galveston hospital. His huge tent was burned to the ground in Temple, Texas, in 1934. Ed. Thardo wrote an account of the fire to his family back home in Odessa:

A lady was driving to Ft. Worth at 1:15 a.m. and she said she saw a man throw a ball of fire on our tent and she put in the alarm. Burnie [Massengale] woke me up hollering the tent is on fire. I run to the front and saw we could not save the top as the fire men had not got there as yet so I run back stage and ordered all the trunks outside. I took the ladies side took out all of them, then grabbed all the wardrobe hanging on the hooks. I got my trunk my clothes and dog out. Then I happened to think my purse was under my mattress 5.00 bucks in it. I got on the stage and the canvas was burning over my head got my purse also my suit case it was starting to burn as I jumped off the stage a side pole hit my bean but didn't do any damage as my head is ivory anyway but I lost my bed and 2 pairs of shoes. One pair was new but I am glad we got all the trunks out. It burned all the canvas and wall. Lost the red plush, blue plush, and silver drops, lots of poles and over 300 chairs are in bad shape. . . . Harley put up a big sign on the lot THE SHOW MUST GO ON. Will show balance of the week at the auditorium and we sure had a nice biz. All the town people are in sympathy with Harley in his big loss.

Loss from the fire was a monumental $12,000, uninsured since the rates were prohibitively expensive. Sadler offered a five hundred dollar reward for information leading to the perpetrator, but no firm information was forthcoming. Perhaps a religious fanatic or a pyromaniac started the blaze, but speculation centered elsewhere. Thardo expressed the commonly held opinion when he wrote to his family, "The picture show done it as sure as you are a foot high."

The following year, gale-force winds struck the show during the first Panhandle engagement of the season. With Claude Kelley no longer bossing the canvas crews, disaster followed, and equipment was spread over what seemed like half of Floyd county. The newspaper related that,

Friday night members of the show company with a lot of volunteer helpers spent two or three hours gathering up scenery, costumes, and other effects and storing them in buildings around town. Saturday most of the men in the show spent repairing wall canvas, while Sadler ordered another top to meet him Monday for his engagement in Plainview.

But the work of Saturday was practically wasted. No matinee show could be given as was planned and threatening clouds of the early evening began a downpour in the second act that drove a large crowd from the improvised air dome [sidewalls without a top] to better cover.

Despite such disasters, Sadler remained optimistic, agreeing with President Herbert Hoover that "Prosperity is just around the corner." Discussing his condition with a reporter about the time of Roosevelt's election, he remarked,

Fate has been kinder to me than I deserve.... In the prosperous years I made large sums of money. Now things are different, but I believe there is a silver lining behind the clouds of depression. I would hate to disband my show and throw a lot of people out of work. I keep holding on, thinking conditions will improve, despite the fact that I have lost a big sum in the last two years.

Clearly Harley was in the grip of The Manager's Disease, an almost incurable malady. A person seized by this affliction suffers from the monomaniacal conviction that his theatre must be kept open at all costs, that upon his shoulders rests the responsibility for maintaining a hallowed artistic tradition. He must provide employment for actors who would starve to death if he did not care for them.

Occasionally, they almost starved to death even with his care. Sue Kelley tells of the time the show was stranded in Galveston, in 1934, flat broke. Harley had gone to West Texas on a borrowing expedition, but was having little luck. He called Sue on long distance, sounding worried: could she feed her husband and his canvas crew until he could find some money?

The resourceful Mrs. Kelley had sixteen hundred carefully hoarded pennies in a lard can, money intended to begin a savings account for Rhoda Lou, the Kelley's baby daughter. No one else in the crew had any cash at all! By purchasing the biggest ham available, laying in sacks of flour and rice, and searching the markets for bruised fruit, she was able to feed this laboring crew of seven, herself and her baby for four days. This was a total of a hundred and eight meals—for sixteen dollars.

For many people during the depression, life on the tent show represented a definite improvement over their state. Olan Burrows was one of the hungry, out-of-work persons who relished the chance that a job with Sadler offered.

Olan was a young man during the early thirties when improved highways made it possible for Sadler to motorize his company. When his uncle leased a truck to the tent show operator, Olan went along as driver. For him, conditions as a crew member were a definite advancement. Sleeping around or under the truck on a regular basis was not regarded as deprivation, nor was bathing in a scrub bucket after sweaty hours of put-up and tear-down. Best of all, crewmen were paid the magnificent sum of $3.00 a day in times when field hands were making 35¢ for picking a hundred pounds of cotton. They had no room rent to pay, and a $5.00 meal ticket could be purchased at a local restaurant for $4.00, with a complete dinner costing no more than fifty or sixty cents.

The job offered more than momentary recompense, for the crew shared in the glamor of show business. Olan, in uniform, marched in front of the street band carrying the Sadler banner, and occasionally appeared as a walk-on in the larger cast plays. "We [the crew] managed to dress so that people would know we were with the show," he recalls, "and we kept our hair long, like the actors."

By 1934, the depression was in full swing, and Billie's diamonds, the security blanket carried by nearly all show people, seemed to journey from one pawn shop to another. At one time, Claude Kelley was put in hock with the diamonds. Melroy, a magician, wanted to take out a large tent and needed a top-flight canvasman; Harley needed money to get his show out of San Antonio. A bargain was struck: Kelley went with Melroy as boss canvasman, Melroy's wife was temporarily adorned with Billie's diamonds, and Harley got a much-needed loan.

A letter from Beaumont, dated January 8, 1935, to the multi-talented Bob Siler reveals to what straits Sadler had come.

Dear Bob:

This will be short and snappy. Galveston was very bad and this has been *even worse, but maybe as soon as they get over their New Year's jag, it will pick up....I think I will trim down considerably and if you would be interested in joining about the 25th of January, I will try to line up something for you. Your salary is going to have to be exceedingly small until things pick up and your duties will be exceedingly large until I can afford to get you some help. This arrangement may not appeal to you but in case it does, I would like to have you. The salary will be $15.00 [a week] to start with. Here are some of your duties. I figure I shall have quite a number of good parts for you in the new rep. I expect I will want you to play saxaphone and maybe sit in on the drums once in a while, have full charge of the props, maybe paint some banners, do some singing and help [put] up and [tear] down. I know that isn't asking a whole lot but I thought it might as well state all of this definitely and clearly so there would be no misunderstanding. I expect it will be a small show for the time being and everybody is going to have to double forty ways.___*

Your friend,

Harley Sadler

Desperate times called for desperate measures. Harley embarked upon a series of money-raising schemes intended to revive his flagging fortunes. In 1935 his friend Phil Isley came into possession of the Bailey Brothers Circus and offered it to Harley for a modest sum. Both believed that the circus could, with the addition of the magical Sadler name, provide a substantial return.

Harley became a ringmaster. Circus-mad since his early youth, he opened the Harley Sadler-Bailey Brothers Circus in Tulsa where it had been stranded; then headed for familiar Texas territory. Billie joined him as business manager, and a scared-to-death Gloria rode an elephant in the opening "spec." Roy E. Fox, Harley's old mentor, came back with his family to manage the still-operating rep show. Harley sent the ever-loyal Paul Thardo-Kalmbacher along as business manager—to see that he was not out-Foxed.

The three-day stand of the circus at Lubbock's South Plains Fair in the autumn was well attended. Featured, according to an advertisement in the *Lubbock Avalanche* were

3 HERDS OF ELEPHANTS
2 BANDS—200 PEOPLE
50 THRILLING ACTS
25 FUNNY CLOWNS

Jack Hoxie, a well-known cowboy actor whose career had

peaked in the mid-twenties, was a featured performer, along with his horse Scout.

According to Phil Isley, the circus did very well at the box office. Little of the proceeds, however, found its way into the depleted coffers of the Sadler enterprises. The road-wise world of circus people was considerably different from the simple, trusting environment of the tent show. Harley was unable to cope with the grifters who siphoned off money as rapidly as it came in. In November, he leased Bailey Brothers to the Goldman Brothers, and in December sold the entire show to Ben Mouton, who had a "perch and fire diving act." Harley's venture under a circus white top lasted only three months.

After this dismal failure, the financially troubled manager launched a grandiose pageant called *The Siege of the Alamo*. Texas' Centennial was to be celebrated in 1936, a propitious time to produce a show which would appeal to native pride in the past. Harley claimed authorship of the *Alamo* script, but he may have been assisted by a New Mexican minister, and perhaps others also had a hand in the writing. At any rate, the result was remarkably forgettable: actors who appeared in this—"turkey" is the only suitable designation—have drawn a blissful veil of oblivion over their usually faultless recollections. Most of them cannot remember what part they played ("I was Santa Anna, I think....or was I Sam Houston?") and no one remembers much about the plot. Only June Mundee, of the juggling team of Mundee and June, knows for sure what part she played. She and her husband were dressed as Indians, and they juggled—what else? Indian clubs!

Some of the confusion resulted from the rewriting and play-doctoring that took place, causing roles to be switched, dropped or changed before the script went into its well-deserved place in the ash heap. Harley may have performed as a red-headed beekeeper, or he may have been the historical character Deaf Smith. A review from the Coleman newspaper, where *Alamo* appeared under the sponsorship of the Business Men's Bible Class, states that "Mr. Sadler takes a minor part in the cast, that of a courier, but as usual has the crowd in stitches with his humorous lines."

At the end of June, Harley took the show to Dallas, against the advice of many members of the company. He may have been remembering his role in *When Toby Hits New York*, where the simple bumpkin triumphs over city sharks and slickers by the application of wholesome,

Paul Thardo-Kalmbacher in costume for Siege of the Alamo.

country goodness. Nature, in this case, did not imitate art.

Harley's was the third Alamo to appear in Dallas that summer. The first had been a replica built for the midway of the city's Centennial Exposition. The other was contained in *Cavalcade of Texas,* a gigantic pageant with thirty-nine scenes and six episodes, which had opened two weeks before Harley's arrival. John Rosenfield, cultural arbitrer of Dallas, had observed in the *Morning News* that *Cavalcade,* in spite of the tendency of the Alamo setting to run off its track, contained sufficient spectacle to carry the production through scheduled two-a-day performances for the rest of the summer.

Aside from the competing Alamos, Sadler faced further, awesome competition for the entertainment dollar. A melodrama company was performing the popular *Drunkard* on a make-believe showboat. A Shakespeare company, under the direction of the renowned Thomas Wood Stevens, was presenting the dramas of the The Bard at a newly constructed Old Globe. Sanger Brothers, a downtown department store, presented *Texas Under Six Flags* on their seventh floor. On the Exposition midway, Midget City was doing stage shows. The Uptown movie theatre featured live vaudeville with the film presentations.

Fleshly delights appeared at the Exposition, probably inspired by Sally Rand's success at Chicago's World Fair in 1933-'34. Mlle. Corrine did her Apple Dance at The Street of All Nations, and amateur night at The Streets of Paris drew enthusiastic audiences.

The week that Harley arrived in Dallas, the Gainesville Community Circus began its run in the Cotton Bowl. In nearby Fort Worth, Billy Rose and John Murray Anderson were at work on another spectacular production, *Frontier Centennial,* scheduled to open in July.

Into the maelstrom of sophistication and sex strolled Harley Sadler and his country players, determined to make it in the big time. The only playing space they could find in this over-entertained community was at the Sportatorium, a wrestling arena.

Apparently, a kind of dinner theatre was planned. The *Dallas Morning News* reported that "a large floor is being built, suitable for any type of entertainment, and the floor is being devoted largely to table seats." Faced with the competition already operating in Dallas, Harley decided that a mere *Alamo* was not enough; he would do a double feature! To his pageant, "with a cast of 100 people," was added "a modern farce comedy, *This Thing Called Love.*"

Even the table service became part of the entertainment. According to the *Morning News,*

The first rehearsal of the thirty-two singing waitresses was held on Sunday afternoon at the Sportatorium. Many novelty numbers are being planned for this innovation in the amusement world of Dallas, and the waitress chorus will sing numbers as they serve refreshments to the patrons of the place.

On July 8th, this potpourri production opened, with prices of 25¢ and 40¢. If critic John Rosenfield attended the performance, he very kindly refrained from printed comment. Two days later the entertainment tried a new format. A tiny one-inch ad appearing on the Amusement page of *The News* outlined the change.

SPORTATORIUM

Tonight and every night
8 to 9—Floor Show
9-11—The Siege of the Alamo
11-12—Vaudeville
12 till ?—Dancing

Music by Henry Santry's Orchestra

According to the route book kept by Bob Siler, the company remained in Dallas for almost a month, but advertisements disappeared from the newspapers after the first week. The entire enterprise was a total disaster. "The actors had to borrow money from each other to buy gas to get out of town," Siler recalls. According to his carefully kept records, *Alamo* played a week in Amarillo and split weeks in Borger and Memphis before disbanding. Many of the performers, including Siler, then joined Roy E. Fox, who had leased the Sadler tent equipment for a sixteen weeks' tour through Fox's old territory in East and Central Texas. The Fox had not lost his cunning: when the show closed in Marshall, Siler was owed a never-collected $180.

The Sadlers, in the meantime, had taken out "Harley Sadler's Society Circus augmented from the London Hippodrome." According to a *Billboard* story, the presentation was "patterned after Billy Rose's *Jumbo* at the Fort Worth Centennial," but in reality it was little more than an indoor dog-and-pony show. Owned in partnership with a

The company for Siege of the Alamo with members of the Roy E. Fox tent show company included. Harley, wearing a straw hat, stands in the middle. Billie is seated slightly to his right beside her mother, Louise Massengale.

man named Tol Teeters, the "circus" featured two elephants, a trained goat act, and performing "alley dogs." Charles Guy, then editor of the *Lubbock Avalanche*, witnessed the presentation at Sled Allen's Auditorium, but failed to see "the quality show that people had come to expect from Harley Sadler." By December, even this modest enterprise had come to an end, Sadler opining that "the territory was just not responsive to this class of show." He and his wife went home to Sweetwater, promising to announce future plans after "doing some resting up."

Although there were still hard times ahead, the closing of the Society Circus represents the bottoming out of Sadler's career. Although his show equipment and comfortable home in Sweetwater had been sold to pay bills, he still owed over $25,000 to a hundred creditors. Moving his family into a small rented cottage, Sadler put his get-rich-quick schemes behind him and set out doing what he could do best: entertaining the people of the crossroads and villages.

After rejecting bankruptcy as a way out of his pressing financial problems, Sadler wrote letters to his creditors promising eventual payment. He rented a ragged little tent outfit for a dollar a day—according to his brother Ferd—and headed for the farmlands of the Lower Valley, playing one-night stands of *Rose of the Rio Grande,* more commonly known as *Sputters,* since its comic lead was a stuttering cowboy. The play was popular even with the largely Spanish-speaking population on the banks of the Rio Grande. A report sent to *Billboard* from the tiny south Texas town of Alamo (the word means "cottonwood" in Spanish) noted that "the show carries a better-than-average band and a neat lineup. Rolling stock is in excellent shape and the show carries its own electric-light plant." A generator would be a necessity, since many of the towns Harley was playing were still lit by kerosene.

According to Ferd Sadler, Harley was ashamed to bring this sorry little show up to his home territory, or even to put his name on the marquee. Playing under the title of The Lone Star Comedians, he was able to save a little money and purchase a better tent and equipment. By 1938 the once again solvent showman was again touring West Texas under his own name.

Sadler never seemed to be concerned with money owed him, but his debts weighed heavily. He once told his brother, "Ferd, I was badly in debt, but I made a list, and as money came in, I'd send so much to this one or that one. By the end of the season [in the Valley] I'd paid them off."

Bob Siler's route book again fills in the narrative. In the winter of 1938 Sadler opened an indoor season of circle stock. For eight trips around the wheel, the actors played two days at Abilene, two in San Angelo, and one each in Big Spring and Sweetwater, with Sunday reserved for rest and church-going. Closing the indoor season, the company opened under canvas on April 12, showing mainly one and two night stands, but with occasional four and six day runs in such population centers as Iowa Park, Lubbock, and Hobbs, New Mexico. By Siler's count, that season they played 112 towns in forty-two weeks.

After recovering his solvency and a measure of self-esteem, Harley was able to look back on the lean years with a certain objectivity. "I was desperate," he told a reporter, "and when the circus was offered me for a song I took it, hoping to recoup financial reverses suffered through the operation of my show. For quick money the circus is tops, but it didn't pan out." The reporter went on to note, "The past two seasons have been successful ones, financially, for the Sadlers. The $25,000 deficit which stared them in the face at the close of 1936 has been wiped out."

"We're out of debt now," Harley said with a smile, "and extremely happy." Later, during his political career, he was introduced at a luncheon as "The first man to make a million dollars from a tent show."

"And the first man to lose a million dollars by the same route," he added wryly.

Chapter Eight

Gloria: Domestic Tragedy

THIS ONLY CHILD of the Sadlers could have turned out much differently than she did. Certainly many of the ingredients which go to form the typical stage brat were present. She was born of reigning tent show stars, named for movie queen Gloria Swanson, began dancing and flashing her dimples before adoring audiences before she had learned to walk properly. She was spoiled shamelessly by her father's employees, treated like a princess by small town audiences, then alternately neglected and over-indulged by parents preoccupied by their own careers. She might have grown into an imperious, demanding child; later a temperamental, unstable performer. Her tempestuous stage career would be attended by a string of disastrous marriages and several unwanted children.

Certainly the young Gloria looked like a good casting for the role. A white rabbit coat, blonde ringlets, and a sparkling, everpresent smile marked her as a child of the theatre. But there were differences, the fur coat (June Havoc once called it the uniform of the stage child) was always a brilliant white, never grayed by restless hours spent in dusty backstages nor sooted-over from fitful naps in dirty day coaches. Her carefully tended curls were a natural honey blonde which deepened naturally as she grew older. The smile was genuine and the flush in her cheeks came not from the makeup box but from Texas sunshine.

Essentially Gloria was a secure child, one who never doubted that she was loved. During her parents' many absences, someone was always ready to take their place. Usually the gap was filled by her grandmother, Mamma Lou Massengale, or Elnora Robison, a black housekeeper who ruled the Sadlers' residence for many years. When Gloria was with the show, any member of the troupe could become temporary parents to the young girl.

Discipline was not lacking. If this littlest Sadler was indulged, she was also required to toe the same mark as the

A young Gloria Sadler poses for a studio portrait.

rest of the company. The tightly structured environment of the traveling community would not allow the disruption caused by a troublesome child. Everyone was expected to earn his keep on the show regardless of age, and Gloria was no exception.

Moreover, she seems to have been born with a sensible, stable personality. Heredity must certainly have been working hand-in-hand with environment to produce a young girl capable of melding easily into almost any situation in which she found herself. Prosperous times or the depression, stable life in a small town or chaotic living in a different town every week—Gloria encompassed them all with apparent ease.

A Negro maid travelled with the family while Gloria was quite small, her chief duty being to care for the small child. Louise Hefner Sorensen remembers prowling the stores of Main Street, always followed by a black shadow dressed in a crisp, blindingly white, maid's costume. "It definitely was a costume," Mrs. Sorensen recalls, "because it served to identify Gloria as the Sadler child." The costume also protected the maid from the abuse that would have greeted a black woman who dared to enter a segregated establishment by herself.

Gloria could not escape from the stage. Tent show offspring took to the stage like ducks to a pond—fortunately, since the dancing child was a recognized feature of the between-acts vaudeville. At the age of three, Gloria was doing specialty numbers during the winter stock season in Houston—and almost ended her career. Her filmy dance skirt came in contact with a backstage stove that helped warm the actors, and instantly she was enveloped in flames. Mamma Lou, her grandmother, smothered the flames with a blanket, but not before her legs and back were seriously burned. As the child was rushed to a hospital, her parents attempted to finish the show.

When the curtain fell on an abbreviated performance, the Sadlers rushed to the hospital to find their tiny daughter lying in the middle of an adult bed, a wire frame supporting the sheet over her burned body. "Look everybody!" she said as her parents rushed into the room, "Now I have a tent like my Daddy."

As Gloria approached school age, her parents bought an attractive, tile-roofed brick house in Sweetwater, apparently seeking a more normal situation for her growing up. During parental absences, her grandmother and Elnora saw that the young girl's clothes were washed and ironed, that there were nourishing hot meals on the table, that the house was clean, and that the flower garden was the envy of all of Sweetwater. Gloria had Rags, an affectionate little dog of indeterminate parentage, and a playroom over the garage which was kept filled with an ever-changing array of dolls and toys.

At first Gloria had trouble adjusting to life with her parents as occasional visitors to the household. In this pre-divorce era when all the other children in Sweetwater had resident mothers and fathers, Gloria felt semi-orphaned. Soon after moving into the house, she dragged a FOR SALE sign onto the front lawn: if the house was sold, she could go back on the road. At night, she often slept with one of Billie's chiffon scarves because, as she said, "It smells like my mother." Others recall her standing at the classroom window in the schoolhouse, watching her home across the street so that she could wave a final goodby to her parents as they left on yet another tour.

Several of Gloria's friends remember the first time they ever saw her. It was at school, in the middle of the year, when this strange child arrived. According to Nancy Fortner Prentiss:

In came this little girl with long blonde hair and a white fur coat. She was the main topic of conversation at recess, but when we found her to be so friendly and not "stuck up" she was soon in the circle. She could sing and dance and we all thought that was great. She was a little chubby . . . in her early days.

Mickey Tubb Rhea's memories are remarkably similar: "She sure was a beautiful child with her blonde curls and big blue eyes. I'm sure the rest of us looked like clods with our straight and banged Buster Brown haircuts."

Mary Paxton Roberts remembers that Gloria, that first year, was the play princess of East Ward School, traveling about during recess on a royal palanquin that looked, to the adult observer, much like an unpainted two by ten.

Everyone used to want to serve as her slave and help carry her wherever she beckoned from the board that we pretended was her golden chariot.

There was never any argument about taking turns as princess—it was just accepted and unquestioned that there was only one the entire school year—because there was only one who qualified.

Like her parents, Gloria has the ability to excel without arousing envy. As Mickey Rhea recalls,

She was always beautiful and yet I can remember no one feeling jealous. Nor was there any jealousy of her talent. In later years we all "performed" at school functions. I'm sure no one thought anything about her outshining us—which she certainly did.... She had a sense of humor, much initiative, and was totally without malice.

Gloria's grandmother was perhaps not the ideal foster-mother for this comparatively sophisticated young girl. A snuff-dipping country woman whose horizons did not extend very far beyond her kitchen and flower beds, Mamma Lou really was not able to comprehend the world of her effervescent granddaughter. Fortunately Gloria's innate sensibleness kept her within the bounds of smalltown propriety.

Although very grown up in some of her attitudes, she could be as silly and giddy and giggly as the other young girls. She had more spending money than most of her friends, and could be counted on to treat for the movies, especially Saturday afternoon horse operas. Gloria adored Indians, and would attend any film that featured Red Men on the lurid showcase posters. But if the action grew scary, if the flames leaped around the heroine as she struggled to free herself from the stake, Gloria would bury her face in her hands. Nancy Prentiss recalls a horrifying *Frankenstein* that put both of them literally *under* the movie house seats.

Gloria's summers were spent with her parents on the show. Having adjusted to a more regular kind of existence, these months of wandering about the country were not what she might have chosen, even though they did mean that she would be with her parents, and that she would become again the crown princess of a tented fairyland. Her circle of girl friends had become as important to her as family; to them she would express her hopes, doubts, worries. "She needed love and attention," Marjorie Stevenson Hager recalls.

On the road, the Sadler daughter proved herself to be a trouper. Georgia Babb recalls Gloria from the early forties, at a time when conditions had reduced the company roster to a bare minimum:

She was sweet, kind, unspoiled, although in every town she had hundreds of people wanting to spoil her, wanting to give her presents. She was very generous, would help people with their wardrobe, would jump in and do a part, would go out front and sell popcorn. She never hesitated to pitch in.... She was the daughter everyone wishes they had.

Like her father, she had a generous streak that bordered on improvidentiality. In good times, everything she owned—toys, clothes, money, even her convertible, that ultimate teen-age status symbol—was shared with her friends. When the family coffers were low (a not infrequent occurrence), she bought her clothes at Woolworth's rather than Nieman-Marcus, but the change had little effect on her lifestyle or outlook.

The young Miss Sadler retained her popularity through high school. She was witty, lively, friendly with everyone, but close friends with only a few. Her grades were good but not exceptional. In an era before "going steady" became epidemic, she dated lots of boys, often imagined herself in love, but was never seriously involved.

"I used to double date with Gloria a great deal," Mary Roberts recalls, "and this was very difficult for me, for she always said such clever things and had such beautiful clothes that I tended to feel rather dull. I don't recall feeling any dislike or jealousy—she was just so likeable."

Graduating from Sweetwater High School, she received a scholarship to Hardin-Simmons College, a small Baptist school in nearby Abilene. In her freshman year she was elected Sweetheart of the HSC Cowboy Band, riding one of the six white horses which preceded the marching band.

Even though she adored horses and parades, show business had very little appeal for the young girl, and in spite of obvious talent and years of experience, talk of New York and Hollywood was shrugged off with little comment. She wanted, above all, a husband and a house full of children; but any career plans were not settled until after her first year at Hardin-Simmons.

That summer, her future was determined by a stomachache which sent her to a Lubbock hospital for an appendectomy. During her convalescence, she and Marjorie Stevenson, a friend, were permitted to watch a caesarian section: for Gloria, the skill and dedication of the surgical team, the miracle of surgical birth, was an apotheosis. She would become a nurse, devote her life to caring for those who needed her. That fall, she enrolled at TCU, where she shared a room with Marjorie and embarked upon the pursuit of an RN degree.

True love—or a reasonable facsimile—found Gloria the following summer, in the form of a Southwest Conference football hero. Mary Roberts remembers that

Gloria, center, rode one of the white horses that preceded the Hardin-Simmons marching band.

...it was vitally important to Gloria to learn to bake a superb cherry pie because that was his favorite. The leaning toward domesticity was so very foreign to Gloria's past interests and we knew she must be very much in love. Lots of pie dough and cherries passed through Grandmother Massengale's kitchen that summer.

Gloria adored her Saturday afternoon hero, but less prejudiced observers were not so easily impressed, one labeling him "a huge, arrogant country boy with too many teeth and a big ego." Their courtship had proceeded to a state of semi-engagement when a teammate of the ground-eating halfback took pity on this naive girl from Sweetwater. There were, he told Gloria, two other sweethearts who were sent pictures, clippings, letters and autographed footballs. On one memorable football weekend, all three girls had come to College Station to see this triple-threat man win another one for the Aggies, and he was able to keep each one ignorant of the existence of the others. Marjorie completes the tale:

She was crushed beyond recovery. She packed up his footballs, pictures, and letters and sent them to his hotel in Fort Worth where the team was staying before the game with TCU. Then she waited all day in her room for him to call and explain. He never called—ever. She packed up and went home, dropping out of school before the end of the semester. Next fall, she went back to Hardin-Simmons.

Her senior year she was elected Bronco Queen, a great honor at HSC. She also met Lieutenant John R. Allen, a West Point man who was receiving his basic flying instruction at nearby Stamford. Within a short time they fell in love and eloped, crossing the narrow Oklahoma Panhandle for a hurried marriage in Liberal, Kansas. The Sadler parents, needless to say, were not overjoyed at such a hasty union; but they were not in a position to exhibit much in the way of moral outrage. How often had a young Gloria listened to joyous accounts of her parents' whirlwind courtship and elopement?

Confirmed Gloria-worshippers predictably concluded that the young lieutenant was not good enough for their goddess, but the marriage seems to have been a very happy one. Harley and Billie, after recovering from their initial shock, bid their new son-in-law welcome to the tribe. The young couple moved a hundred miles north to the Lubbock training command, and within a few months Gloria was blissfully pregnant. As her confinement approached, she returned to Sweetwater, planning to have her first baby among family and friends.

"If anything were to happen to her, I don't think I could stand it," Billie said to a friend shortly before Gloria went to the hospital.

Something did happen; just what cannot be determined. She had a long labor, and may have refused a caesarian for fear she would not be able to have any more children. There were many rumors: blood clot, gangrene, congestive heart failure, a wrong injection—no one knows the precise cause, but the result was the same: Gloria and her baby were dead. "Her little heart just stopped," said Harley brokenly. This beautiful adored, twenty-one-year old was simply no more.

Her funeral was emotional, dramatic; Sweetwater's First Baptist Church overflowed with mourners. A soloist sang *My Devotion,* a popular tune that was Gloria's favorite, accompanied by the organ which the Sadlers had donated to the church. The congregation sang with feeling, "If I can help somebody along the way, then my living shall not be in vain."

I distinctly remember her once saying she hoped she would die before she became old and ugly and she described herself as a youthful corpse with hands gracefully enfolding a lily at her breast. I projected a very vivid picture of the beautiful Gloria in this final scene. Because it came from her it did not seem a particularly morbid or uwholesome thought—just dramatic and beautiful.

Gloria's fifteen-year-old flight of fancy as imparted to Mary Roberts came true.

The young Lieutenant Allen, bound to the Sadlers by a shared grief, remained a member of the family. In 1944, two years after Gloria's passing, Billie visited him in California shortly before the Air Force officer was sent overseas. In 1947 Captain Allen with his wife Donnie, and son, Junior, came to see the Sadlers in Perryton, where they were on tour. "Allen has kept in close contact with the Sadlers since their daughter and his wife, Gloria, passed away several years ago," a story in *Billboard* noted. A few years ago, Colonel Allen retired after a career in the United States Army.

The Sadlers were desolated by their loss. They had survived good times and bad, but this blow was too cruel, too unexpected for them to rebound completely. Gloria had promised her father a grandson, and when the family doctor asked Harley whether he wanted to determine the sex of the unborn child, he shook his head. "I couldn't stand to know," he replied.

Harley's grief was insurmountable. He was a righteous

man, who, like Job, found the hand of God turned against him. Job-like, he cried out "Show me my guilt, O God!" Always a Bible reader, he turned more and more to the Scriptures, searching for some reason for Gloria's loss. The ironic utterances of the preacher in *Ecclestiastes* gave him some consolation: "All is vanity," he used to say with as much bitterness as he could summon up. Eventually he found the sin for which he was being punished. "I put her before God," he told his brother Ferd. "I worshipped her to the point of idolatry."

Billie could find no such reason for the loss of her beloved child. She did find, though, that alcohol would relieve, for a time, the aching void in her heart. Although she had never been immune from occasional overindulgence, her serious problems with alcohol date from the time of Gloria's death.

The sorrowing parents dedicated themselves to keeping memories of Gloria alive, as though this somehow lessened her passing. Four years after their loss, Marian McKennon recalls that in her first encounter with the Sadlers, "You met Gloria as you met Billie and Harley. She was always in their thoughts and conversation." Gil Lamb, the now-reformed black sheep from earlier days, renewed his acquaintance with Harley in 1947 when the show was playing Lubbock. Although the showman had important late-evening appointments with politicians and oil associates, he cancelled them all to spend the evening with Lamb in a hotel room, reminiscing about Gloria.

Gloria was never forgotten. Twice a week, flowers were put on the Massengale family plot in Cameron, and every week on the anniversary of her death, the grave was blanketed in gardenias. Annually, a two-column remembrance appeared on the rep page in *Billboard*. Usually it contained a picture of a happy, smiling Gloria, sometimes a few lines of poetry, and often the closing phrase, "Darling, you are constantly in our thoughts."

Chapter Nine

New Roles: Oil and Politics

WITHIN THE PAST THIRTY YEARS, the entertainer seems to have found the field of politics not as inhospitable as it had once been. Song-and-dance man George Murphy has been elected to the United States Senate, as has Texas showman-huckster W. Lee "Pappy" O'Daniel. Cowboy star Tex Ritter and radio personality Gordon "The Old Scotchman" McClendon made nearly successful bids for Senate Seats. Jimmy Davis, composer of "You Are My Sunshine," became Governor of Louisiana, and movie actor Ronald Reagan, after service as Governor of California, was elected to the Presidency of the United States. Such public acceptance of the entertainer has not always been so: certainly Roy E. Fox lost little sleep pondering his decision not to stand for Governor of Texas. After all, who ever heard of a tent showman running for anything but the county line?

Since the beginning of the depression, Harley Sadler heard his name mentioned in barber shop political discussions, but he always scoffed at any suggestion that he run for office. "After all," he told his brother Ferd, "I'm not an educated man. I've never been to college, studied the law." Nevertheless, he seemed to be destined to play a role in politics.

His first foray into the political arena came as a speech maker for Jerry Sadler, an unknown who asked his aid in a race for the Texas Railroad Commission, a powerful regulatory body which controls oil production within the state. If Jerry was any kin at all to the popular showman, it was an extremely distant relationship; but Harley generously claimed the candidate as a "cousin," and a great many voters actually believed that they were brothers. Harley's participation in the campaign was limited to making an occasional speech on Jerry's behalf, putting up posters outside his tent, and giving Jerry a brief boost during his between-acts homily. Harley's vote-getting potential was little short of astounding: his almost unknown shirt-tail "cousin" won an impressive coattail victory.

147

Oilman Sadler, his face covered by a wide grin, watches as an exploration well is brought in at Goat Hill, near Coleman, Texas. The joy was short-lived: before an offset well could be completed, the original had gone dry.

Two years later, the new Railroad Commissioner made a bid for the Governor's mansion, and again Harley joined his campaign forces. Although Jerry lost badly in this contest, voting patterns confirmed the power that his Cousin Harley exhibited at the ballot box. Jerry's few respectable tallies in the voting coincided exactly with the route followed by the Sadler show.

About this time, 1940, the successful showman began a new career as an independent oil operator/driller. Just how he drifted into oil exploration is not clear, but very probably a friend offered him an interest in a successful wildcat; he made a quick, very substantial profit from a small investment—and was immediately addicted to a kind of gambling which offered astronomical odds. At any rate, the fraternity of independents welcomed Harley into their midst, and he was soon immersed in arcane discussions of rights and leases, pools, synclines, acidization and core samples. In essence, wildcatting was not much different from the backstage crap games that Harley loved so much—except that stakes were higher, odds were steeper, and Mother Earth was the croupier.

As with most gamblers, he won a few rolls, but lost quite a lot more. "Call me Dry-Hole Sadler," he once sardonically replied to a reporter's query. Former Governor Preston Smith recalls a near bonanza in which he and the diminutive showman were involved. Sharing a shallow exploration east of Coleman, they were able to bring in a good producer, and it seemed as though Lady Luck had smiled upon them.

The smile turned out to be only a grimace caused by a transient gas pain. Resisting several lucrative offers to sell out their interests, the Smith-Sadler combine began a second drilling: before the offset well could reach oil-bearing strata, the original exploration had gone totally, permanently dry.

Maurice Brookes, an Abilene attorney, recalls another time when he and Harley were eating a lunch of sardines and soda crackers at a country store near a drilling site. The phone rang, and over the crackling party line could be heard the voice of a California millionaire who had a financial interest in this exploration. "How's it going?" he enquired.

Harley, after managing to shift a mouthful of dry crackers into his cheek, cleared his throat, and opined, "Seems as if we're the owners of a nine barrel well."

"Drill it deeper," barked the voice on the telephone, and Harley rang off with a loud sigh. Later, in Abilene, Brookes asked what happened with the well.

"We drilled it deeper ... and deeper ... and finally we let in the whole Gulf of Mexico," the novice oilman replied.

In common with most independent operators, the once-successful showman found himself chronically overextended and not infrequently near bankruptcy. There were occasional producing strikes which brought in a flood of dollars, but then a series of "dusters" would dry up the flow.

Harley was not well equipped to deal with shrewd manipulators: all his life, he remained more than a little naive, a little too trusting. Of course, there was always a group of people who, perceiving his innocence and lack of guile, did their best to protect him from waiting predators. There were also many ordinary citizens who loved Harley and tried to work for his benefit—but could not resist the temptation to skim a little from box office receipts, pad a due-bill knowing the itemization would never be checked, forget a debt owed, or crawfish out of a dry hole deal where the only contract consisted of a nod and a handshake. The temptation to take advantage of such a person was almost irresistible, especially so since he never seemed to hold a grudge or thirst for revenge.

In an effort to transform himself into a successful businessman, Harley kept the show off the road in 1940, leasing his outfit to Jack Turner. When the company, which included many Sadler regulars, limped back to Sweetwater after a disastrous tour of a one-nighter called *South of the Border,* Sadler could not resist the opportunity to go back on the road for what remained of the season.

By this date, the large tent shows with companies of fifty had vanished, and the few still operating were only shadows of the good old days. Company rosters had shrunk so drastically that everyone was tripling and quadrupling in assignments. *Billboard* reported that Sadler, besides playing comedy leads and serving as emcee, was playing drums for the vaudeville. In addition, "Manager Sadler ... presides as boss canvasman, chief electrician, and head truck driver.... Billie Sadler sees the family trailer through."

Obviously, the days of the tent show were over. Once, they had been the means of escaping the unbearable temperatures of indoor auditoriums during the summer months, but now that movie theatres had discovered the magic of refrigerated air, even tent show actors could be found on summer afternoons luxuriating in the cool darkness of the cinema. By 1940, drive-in theatres were proving successful, capturing a further share of the tent show audience, particularly younger people with new families.

Sadler did what he could to stay abreast of the times. When the highly successful Grand Ole Opry, heard over Nashville radio station WSM, added several touring revues under canvas to their production schedule, the Sadler vaudeville turned increasingly to hillbilly routines and country music. Searching for the formula for success at the box office, he opened two country variety shows on the Midway at Texas' State Fair in 1941, but neither was successful enough to warrant reopening the following year.

In that same year, he opened an elaborate, semi-permanent show near a newly established army training camp at Brownwood, perhaps remembering the success he had enjoyed playing to doughboys in Texas City at the start of World War I. Such niceties as a neon marquee, gravelled walkways, and piped-in gas heating added to a musical revue format should have delighted entertainment-starved GIs. However, only 18% of the slim audiences wore khaki: this was a more sophisticated movie-raised generation. These citizen-soldiers, uprooted mainly from urban locations in the East and Midwest, were not interested in cornball country entertainment—no matter how boring existence could be in this remote Texas town.

Failing to lick the movies, Sadler decided to join them. Forming a partnership with Phil Isley, he opened a film theatre named The Sadler, in Kileen, near Fort Hood. This proved so successful that a second house was opened nearby, with a third being added in Temple shortly thereafter. While Harley shared in the profits of these theaters, management remained in the hands of Isley, who owned many movie houses throughout the state.

In 1942, shortly after Pearl Harbor, friends prevailed upon the showman to run for the State Legislature. Surviving a run-off election in the Democratic primary, he was elected to the House of Representatives from the Sweetwater area. That same year, after an unsuccessful tour with his little tent company, Representative Sadler announced in *Billboard* that he was folding his tent permanently. Considering the wartime restrictions upon travel, the demands of his oil operations, and new responsibilities in the Legislature, this was the only sensible course to pursue. However, performers have never been noted for being sensible; the following year, Sadler was back on the road.

In 1943, the year the fifty-one year old showman began serving in the House, he unexpectedly volunteered for the army. In the First World War, showmen such as W.I. Swain were able to teach the army something about the logistics of moving tented cities, but this was a war of quonset huts, not canvas bivouacs; Harley's request for a commission was evidently refused.

Undaunted by this rejection, he took out his tent for a highly successful War Bond tour. *Ravaged Earth,* a propaganda film, was presented, together with speeches by local organizations promoting bond purchases. Expenses of the tour were borne by Sadler.

Gloria died in October of 1943, and her grief-stricken father immediately sold all his show equipment to Jam-Up and Honey, stars of the Grand Ole Opry. He resolved not to stand for re-election to the "Ledge," but friends filed for him and then persuaded him to allow his name to remain on the ballot. Without campaigning, he carried that election by a two-to-one margin.

About four months after Gloria's death, her father began having second thoughts about the wisdom of attempting to retreat into a world of private sorrow. Harley was a gregarious person who had probably never eaten a meal alone in his life; now, with Gloria's passing, he needed friends around him more than ever. The tent show would place him again at the hub of a busy little universe, where he would have little time for private reflection. Too, the busy life of trouping would be excellent therapy for Billie, who was having severe problems adjusting to life without her adored child.

Buying part of his equipment from the Madden-Stillian Players, of Lake City, Iowa,* and the remainder from the widow of J. Doug Morgan, an East Texas showman, Harley put together enough of an outfit to get back on the road by late spring of 1941. Soon, he was battling the blustery weather of the Panhandle. "SRO AND WIND," captioned

---

*A recent letter from Dale R. Madden Sr. gives the following details concerning the purchase: "I never met Harley Sadler unfortunately, but I did sell him a complete tent outfit, and the manner in which we negotiated would indicate to me Harley must have been a beautiful person. As I recall, he telephoned me and asked would I sell him the outfit (I was going in the

Harley used his tent to show propaganda films during World War II.

Billboard. "BIG WEEK IN HEREFORD." "SADLER BEATS WIND TO RACK UP FAIR BLITZ IN TEXAS TERRITORY." "HARLEY SADLER BEATS TEXAS HEAT." "AMARILLO PANS BIG FOR SADLER'S TROUPE." Things were just like they were in the good old days—almost: "SADLER'S TENT IS PATCHWORK NOW" one newspaper headlined. The show and crowds were smaller, players and audiences were older, Gloria was gone. While the show proved good medicine for Harley, Billie was not helped by it. In July, her position as bookkeeper ticket-seller was taken over by G. Bert Davis, an old trouper who had toured under his own banner at one time. "Billie is tired, needs a rest," was the announcement made.

About the time that Billie's drinking problem was becoming severe, Harley was learning of the medicinal properties of alcohol. A chronic sufferer from a nervous stomach, he began taking an evening's dram on doctor's advice. Bob Siler remembers the showman standing in front of the bathroom mirror with a measured dose of bourbon, choking it down and complaining about the "nasty-tasting stuff." But as he became acclimated to the political life of the State Capitol, the fledging law-maker learned to carry a highball in his hand through unavoidable cocktail parties— and occasionally to drink it!

Billie's drinking was another matter. Her increasingly serious alcoholism was one matter that was never discussed. People knew that Billie drank, and Harley knew that they knew; but a barrier of silence surrounded the subject. Worried friends discussed the matter among themselves, but Harley, so frank and open on most matters, never joined in these talks. This remained his personal cross.

Billie was a middle-aged, suddenly and tragically childless woman who had fallen into the grip of an addictive drug. Alcoholism was not recognzied as a disease in the 1940s; indeed for many West Texans, drink was a temptation sent by the devil himself, and anyone who partook automatically fell from the ranks of the annointed. There

---

Army at the time). I agreed to sell to him, we established a price, and he said in so many words: Well Dale, sent it to me, I am mailing you a check immediately. I suggested that perhaps he would like to see the equipment, but he said Oh no, if you say it is O.K. it will be alright with me. Now I had never met Harley, and he was so pleasant and cooperative about this deal that I have always thought he must have been a fine honest man."

were no social agencies, no counselors, no organization like Alcoholics Anonymous to help people like Billie in their lonely struggle.

Harley's wife fought a losing battle against her addiction. Ferd Sadler recalls how proudly she would report to him that she had been without a drink for two weeks, a month, sometimes even six weeks. But inevitably the temptation would come again, and she could not resist it. Harley, according to Ferd, would become angry, threaten to divorce his wife of over thirty years. Tearfully, Billie would beg a forgiveness that was always granted.

Family tensions were eased when Harley found a "child" to fill some of the void left by Gloria's passing. This occurred when the ever-popular showman was "drafted" for a War Bond tour. An Air Force hero, named with incredible aptness, Norman Bonds, was part of the fund-raising troupe, together with former Texas Governor Jimmy Allred. Bonds recalls that,

After we had been together about a week, Harley would introduce me to the people ... as his adopted son. He did tell me that it would be easier to call him Dad than to say Mr. We seemed to just fall into this pattern. He was a very gracious and affectionate person. Mr. Allred seemed to enjoy our feelings because he told me of Gloria and that Harley seemed his old self.

After his discharge from the Air Force, Bonds moved to Abilene with his wife and a young daughter who called the showman/legislator "Granddaddy." Harley helped to establish the young veteran in a business, and was pleased when two later daughters of the Bonds (they had hoped for one boy) were named Harley Anne and Billie Suzanne.

Politics, which came to fill an ever-increasing part of Harley's life, brought him to a strange environment. The Texas Legislature attracts an unusual group of people: salaries are too low to appeal to the career-minded individual, so what rewards there are must be other than wages. Many independently wealthy individuals serve in the Legislature, millionaires who can afford the financial sacrifice attached to their service. There are a number of short-term lawyers who find that a hitch or two in the Ledge will enhance their practices. Others see the State Capitol as a training ground for the national scene; probably a few venal creatures view these elective offices as an opportunity to feed at the public trough. Some others are motivated by an urge to reform, and some seem to enjoy the exhilaration of the game of politics.

An aging Sadler was still playing the silly kid Toby roles during World War II.

Sadler fit none of these molds. In much the same way that he viewed his tent show as fulfilling a mission to bring wholesome entertainment to his audiences, he regarded election to public office as an opportunity to work for the welfare of his constituents. In his first campaign in 1943 he stated:

I have never before sought public office and do so at this time without any great ambition, but rather through a desire to be of service to the good people of the 117th district.

The freshman legislator approached his new career with a great deal of humility and a certain amount of awe. Realizing the handicaps presented by his scanty education and lack of legal background, he compensated by working diligently, doing his homework on bills, resolutions, committees, appointments. For several years, he had a perfect roll call attendance in the House.

Nothing was too unimportant to him: he would often spend hours trying to find why a bureaucratic decision had cut some poor pensioner's allotment from $40 to $32 a month. As an independent oil man, he was very much concerned with the continuing efforts of the "majors" to gobble up the little operator, and he did what he could to protect the rights of the independents. But he was not a one-note special interest legislator. "I'll vote for any bill that is good for my district or for the whole state of Texas," he said on one occasion.

Former Governor Preston Smith, Sadler's desk-mate for several terms when they were both in the House, states with conviction,

Harley's voting record was as near to actually representing the people as any man I ever served with. He wanted to do exactly what was right. Sometimes he was misled, but not often. .... My belief is that if anyone who served in the Legislature ever voted with the best interests of the people, it would have been Harley Sadler.

Representative Sadler was careful not to become beholden to the hordes of lobbyists who descended like a plague of locusts upon Austin every session. No one had ever been known to pick up a restaurant tab when Harley was in the party, and he continued this practice during his political career. Many lobbyists found it a unique experience to have a legislator take *them* to lunch. Once, according to his brother Ferd, an old friend-turned-lobbyist offered him

$10,000 to change his vote on a crucial piece of oil legislation. "I am not deceived at the ruthlessness of politicians," Harley told a reporter.

Even in a ruthless environment, the fledgling politician retained his innocence, remaining simple and uncomplicated. He was never able to pursue a devious path, regardless of the ultimately meritorious goal to be accomplished. The horse-trading of politics, the mutual back-scratching, vote-swapping, balancing of influences— these were matters he never really comprehended. Like the dramas he had spent most of his life presenting, legislation was a simple matter of right and wrong. After he had studied a bill, discussed it with interested parties, submitted it to the Lord in prayerful consideration, he would vote as his conscience dictated.

Arriving at a decision was always difficult because he operated not from ironclad conviction of his own, but on the basis of arguments presented to him. Always willing to listen to another view, his outlook often shifted from day to day. "Harley's opinion," declared a legislator who served with him, "depended upon who had talked to him last."

Even with his lack of experience, Sadler's work in the Legislature was impressive. During his third year in the Texas House, columnist Raymond Brooks had the following to say in the *Austin American*:

One might assume that this long career [on the stage] would make a confirmed showman of a man, in the sense that he would be acting, or conducting himself in a theatrical manner all the time. Or that he would be extra-sophisticated and cynical, or maybe rough in his expressions.

If anyone should have the idea of the actor-show owner-lawmaker from West Texas, a brief visit to the House of Representatives would correct it.

There has never been a milder, more sincere sort of man in the Legislature than Harley Sadler, within the memory of the old-timers of the press corps. Actually, he has a reserved attitude toward his work in his public office, and a sincere, straightforward considerateness for the other members that permeates all he does and says.

Harley served three terms from the 117th district, a total of six years. His popularity was such that, for his third campaign, the total expenditure of funds was listed as $3.00.

Running for office in West Texas at this time consisted mainly in attending small political rallies held in conjunction with church socials, charity benefits, 4-H or Future Farmers fund-raising events. Audiences were spared elaborate speechmaking, limiting each candidate who appeared to a few offhand remarks. Harley was a master politician in such situations, speaking in the quiet tones he had always used for the between-acts talks on his show, establishing an immediate rapport with his listeners. Within the first minute, he was no longer speaking; he was having a conversation with a few old friends, and heads would begin to nod in agreement as he made his points.

As part of the fund-raising, pies and cakes were auctioned off at these affairs, and defeat awaited the candidate for sheriff or commissioner who was not prepared to outbid his opponent. Harley usually found himself in the enviable position of auctioneer, and he delighted in seeing how much money he could wring from the perspiring bidder-candidates. As auctioneer, Harley was immune from this genteel extortion, but nothing could restrain his generosity. Preston Smith recalls one such gathering where the showman volunteered to pay off a $400 debt on a new church piano—when he was running unopposed. "And at that time, Harley didn't have that kind of money," the former Governor added.

In 1946, after losing a very half-hearted race for Speaker of the House, a powerful position for which he was poorly suited, Harley was urged by friends to run for a seat in Congress. According to former newspaper editor Charles A. Guy, the Sweetwater legislator was "thunderstruck.... 'What business have I in the councils of the mighty?' he inquired."

Another group offered to finance his campaign for Governor against incumbent Buford Jester, whose popularity was waning at the time. Again, Harley said "No," offering "business interests and not too good health" as reasons for declining. To his brother Ferd he said, "I'll run for Governor when I can finance my own campaign, not before."

Having passed up opportunities to move up to Washington or into the Governor's mansion, Harley was destined to go down to an ignominious defeat in a modest effort to move up from the Texas House to the Senate, losing badly to incumbent Pat Bullock. At least part of the reason for this loss can be attributed to Harley's obliging habit of introducing almost any piece of legislation that a friend thrust upon him, dropping it into the House hopper with the thought that more serious consideration would be given when the bill came to a vote.

In this manner, Representative Sadler became notorious as the villain who proposed to take the tractor gas rebate away from farmers and ranchers who, by time-honored custom, were exempt from paying highway taxes on gasoline used for off-highway purposes such as plowing, fencing and feeding. Each year, rural dwellers filed a form which rebated four cents on each gallon of gas used for farm or ranch purposes. This often amounted to a several hundred dollar windfall for each household.

Harley apparently did favor some change in the allocation of the gas taxes, wanting a portion of it to go for education. According to former Senator Bullock the tractor gas issue had been used throughout the campaign, with increased emphasis as voting time drew near. Harley felt misrepresented, and purchased large newspaper ads complaining about "LAST MINUTE, DESPERATE, MUD SLINGING HALF TRUTH POLITICAL TACTICS." He wrote heatedly,

In the closing minutes of this campaign, written and printed material is being circulated which either charges or implies that Harley Sadler favors taking the four cents tractor gas exemption away from the farmers. THIS STATEMENT OR IMPLICATION IS RIDICULOUS, UNFAIR AND UNTRUE.

True or not, tractor gas cost Harley the election. Bullock won by 4,800 votes, his largest plurality. In a statement thanking his supporters, the loser sounded uncharacteristically bitter:

I regret that in the closing hours of this campaign misleading information was distributed through the U.S. Mail and cleverly designed newspaper ads. The returns of the election established these tactics resulted in causing me to lose the vote of many of the type of people with whom I have had my most intimate relationships throughout my life and for whom I have always attempted to work for their best interests. Except for this, I have no regrets.

The acrimony that may have been generated by this hard-fought campaign quickly evaporated. Four years later, when Senator Bullock retired from the Senate, he campaigned vigorously to see that Sadler assumed the seat he was vacating.

Shortly after losing to Bullock, Harley and Billie left Sweetwater, moving forty miles east to the larger town of Abilene. The move may have been partly motivated by an impulse to leave the 117th district that he had represented, but there were other factors. Abilene was a center of oil exploration activity, and a much better place for Sadler to establish his headquarters. But according to one close acquaintance, the chief reason for his departure was the decision by the Sweetwater town council to grant a zoning variance which would allow a funeral parlor to begin operation in Harley's quiet residential neighborhood. He was incensed by the yielding attitude of the council, and although Gloria had been dead for five years, each funeral would be another reminder of her passing. Harley could not endure a daily display of grief being paraded past his front door.

In 1950, having become established in Abilene, he was again elected to the Texas House, and two years later became a candidate for the Senate. As primary time approached, his opposition wilted, and he ran unopposed. Because of redistricting, he drew a short two-year term, standing for reelection in 1952.

In 1951, he talked to an Abilene group about the problems of serving in the State Capitol. "I wish every person could serve in the Legislature, to see what goes into the hopper, its modus operandi, the pressure elements," he said. After a lifetime dedicated to pleasing people, he now found himself in a position where his decisions would inevitably make someone unhappy. "Sometimes I get blue and discouraged," he continued, "I try to be nonpartisan. Since 1943, when I went into politics some of my best friends don't like what I did and it hurts me."

The tendency toward centralization worried him. "We're losing our home governments to Austin. I hope we don't lose local control of our schools." He found no answer to the politician's typical dilemma: "The policy today is to cut taxes but get more things. In Congress every member wants to lop the tax but get a post office."

He was particularly concerned with the penal system and the possibilities of genuine rehabilitation. He visited the state prison at Huntsville and liked what he saw.

The prisoners work as if they were getting $10 a day.... Men quit maiming themselves, there are no riots, 7,000 acres are productive, the system has 10,000 cattle and 5,000 hogs—the finest you ever saw. The system is processing these men, teaching them trades and turning them loose to make good citizens.

In general, Harley could be described as a middle-of-the-road legislator, reflecting the basic conservatism of the area he represented. His colleagues nicknamed him "The Quiet Senator." He lived simply in Austin, with a room at the Washington Hotel. Every evening, as the dining room was closing, he would fill his Thermos bottle with coffee that was being drained from the large urn. Getting free coffee appealed to a usually well-hidden streak of thriftiness, and being an early riser, the hot—if sometimes bitter—brew was pleasant to wake up to. At the same time, that he was saving pennies on stale coffee, ten dollar bills were being handed to maitre d's for service in crowded dining rooms. Friends, chance acquaintances, and total strangers were always able to get a "loan" if they could get the Senator's ear.

Joe Pickle was a West Texas boy who had spent part of every summer as a spectator under Sadler's tent. When he became a political reporter in the Capitol, he found himself placed under Harley's special protection. As he recalled in a retrospective article written shortly after the showman's death,

Part of the beat was to check in at Senator Sadler's office every morning. In contrast to some, I always found him busy at his desk. A lot of it, I discovered, was the sort of business he might just as well have spared himself but didn't. These were the numerous calls of people wanting some personal favor, a job, a recommendation, an introduction to a key official, or like as not a five spot to tide someone over until a payday that was never to be.

One Sunday morning, the young reporter from the *Big Spring Herald,* having slept through the alarm, wandered down to the hotel lobby, intending to skip his usual churchgoing. He met Senator Sadler coming out of the coffee shop and, although still unbreakfasted, found himself gently led to a nearby funeral home which doubled as a Sunday School. The adult group was taught by Governor Shivers, and Sadler confided to the young reporter that he "always gets such a blessing out of the lesson and the class . . . and he wanted me to share it." Later, there were services at the nearby First Baptist Church, and then Sunday dinner at the hotel. The Senator wanted to talk.

He spoke of Gloria, Harley and Billie's only child. . . . I realized how their whole life was wrapped up in Gloria, and how paralyzing was the blow when she and the baby had died at childbirth. . . . "All Billie and I had left was our faith," he said.

I sensed that Harley was in one of his periods of bad luck. Adroitly as my training had taught me, I eased a question in here and there and pieced a

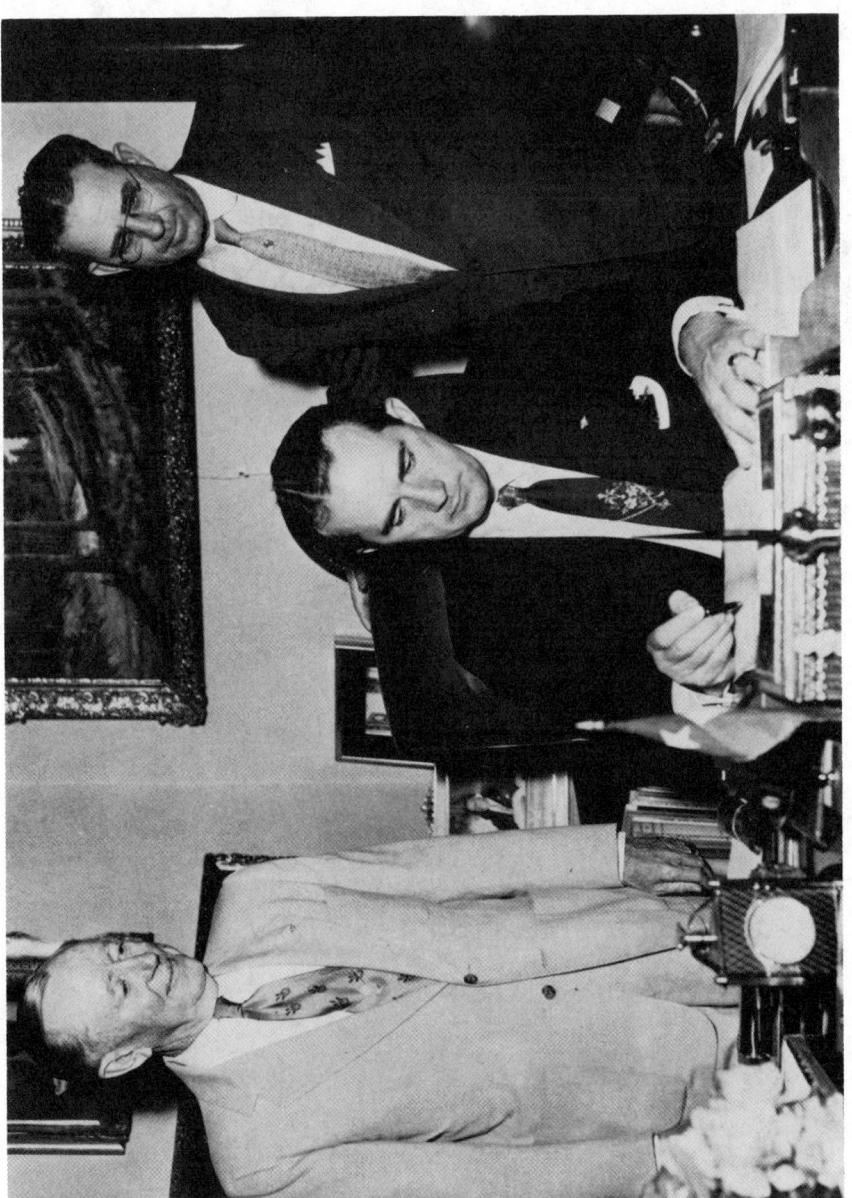

Senator Sadler stands by deferentially as Governor Allan Shivers signs a Sadler-sponsored bill. The House sponsor stands at the right of the Governor.

pattern in my mind of failure upon failure of oil wells until most of his resources had neared exhaustion. Billie was operating a drive-in theatre, and that was the sole bright spot of the family fortunes. But in casual conversation, you would never dream he wasn't riding the crest of good fortune.

I asked the waitress for the check. "Oh," she said almost tolerantly, "Senator Sadler's already taken care of that."

In 1954, Sadler achieved his final political victory, winning renomination for his senate seat in the Democratic primary, the equivalent of election in a one-party state. Probably he had risen to his proper level in the political hierarchy, one which best suited his abilities and desires. "I have rendered conscientious and honest service to the best of my ability," he had said in announcing his candidacy.

Only death ended that service.

Chapter Ten

The Farewell Tour—With a New Partner

JOE MCKENNON WAS—and still is—in many ways the antithesis of Harley Sadler. Harley was small, fragile, winsome, gentle. Joe is a powerful person, and even in his seventies carries about him the air of repressed violence. He always seems on the verge of explosion, so that even a casual conversation with him is, in the words of playwright Langdon Mitchell, "like having tea on the slopes of a volcano."

Two more opposite personalities are hard to imagine. Even more difficult is visualizing two such men becoming friends, finding they could work together as equal partners within the close confines of a tent show—even with totally different approaches to management. Harley governed his troupes by instilling love and gratitude, by encouragement and gentle guidance. Joe ruled by being bigger and stronger than anyone else, by breaking heads when necessary. Harley was the defenseless lamb who brought forth protective instincts in those beneath him. Joe was king of the jungle, and when he roared the lesser creatures sought cover.

McKennon was nearing forty years of age before his first major encounter with dramatic repertoire. A Texas boy raised in Cleburne, he had run away with the circus after serving an apprenticeship as coachmaker on the Santa Fe Railroad. He is, in his own words, "tent simple," loving anything that takes place under canvas. For the rugged McKennon, circus, carnival, and tent show possess an almost equal fascination. He loves not so much what happens inside the tent as the complex operation of this peregrinating village; the logistics of transporting people, animals, housing, kitchens, equipment, scenery, rigging from place to place. The creative thrill of causing this portable theatre to sprout magically from a barren plain, and the destructive satisfaction of tearing it down at every move—these were McKennon's reasons for existing.

Joe's life under canvas did not begin in the cooperative, work-together family environment of the tent rep show. He was blooded in the harsh, sweating, behind-the-scenes work of carnivals and circuses. Quickly rising to a position of authority, he worked as head usher, canvas boss and superintendent on a dozen shows, including Sells-Floto and Ringling Brothers and Barnum and Bailey. Typically, his crews were the dregs of the entertainment world: drifters, misfits, alcoholics, sociopaths. As boss, the young McKennon's task was to drive, bully, wheedle and beat this motley crew into working submission, and to see that the canvas city and all its paraphernalia went up and down with dispatch. He was The Man, the hated symbol of authority, and like most circus and carnival bosses, he kept a trusted worker with him at all times, insurance against being hit in the back of the head with a tent stake.

McKennon's association with dramatic tent shows came about partially as a result of his marriage to Marian Leigh Cross, whom he met during World War II while ramrodding a special army training unit in the searing heat of the California desert. The new Mrs. McKennon did not bear any strong resemblance to the carnival and circus women. She described herself in the following terms:

I am a small woman with reddish-brown hair walloped in braided buns on the back of my head.

After a childhood spent in the "best" schools interlaced with vacation trips abroad with my family, I began to seriously study art. I can never remember when I didn't love to paint, draw, and model. I was a hope-to-be rising portrait sculptor when I married. Even producing two dark, beautiful, sturdy children didn't take me far from my studio.

I had been a widow for seven years, and had moved from Boston to Pasadena, California, when I met Joe.*

This "lady" (a designation she dislikes but accepts resignedly) met her future husband while working as a volunteer aide in a Southern California hospital. Seeming barely half Joe's impressive size, she was able to gentle—or perhaps "civilize" is a better word—this rough, driving man.

*This passage is taken from Marian McKennon's *Tent Show* (New York, 1964), an interesting view of life with a traveling rep company as seen by a "First-of-May boss lady." The account began as a series of letters to Howard Lindsay, who suggested that they be put into book form.

Knowing that she could not compete with her husband's first love, she wisely chose to join him in his adoration of this heathenish idol made of canvas, poles, stakes and rigging.

However, both the McKennons realized that circus or carnival life was not for such "First-of-May" newcomers as Marian and her two children. A dramatic tent show loomed as a possible compromise between tent-worship and art. Howard Lindsay, a friend of the couple, suggested a further compromise: Why not take Broadway to the hinterlands; tour contemporary comedies using a canvas theatre?

Lindsay, a highly successful Broadway playwright with such hits as *Life With Father* to his credit, had been a tent rep actor for a brief period early in his career, and saw possibilities for turning the folksy, family-style tent company into something more nearly resembling the New York theatre. With his help, the McKennons set about planning a show which would use Broadway plays, actors from New York and Hollywood, reserved seats which were *actually* reserved, and even uniformed usherettes. Equipment was to be brand-new, featuring many creature comforts that had never before been provided in this canvas environment. There were even portable toilets, a modern convenience that had never before been seen on a tent show!

The Marian McKennon Dramatic Players opened in the spring of 1946 at Paris, Tennessee, the home of Joe's parents. Three contemporary comedies—*Arsenic and Old Lace, Over Twenty-One* and *Kiss and Tell*—were put into repertoire. This meant that, barring possible holdovers, a three-night stand was possible before moving on to the next location. "BROADWAY COMES TO MAIN STREET," the posters proclaimed. There was a problem, however: Main Street was not much inclined to come to Broadway. "We didn't realize," Marian McKennon wrote, that the bill "would sound snooty to people in little towns. We thought people wanted to see the good, talked-about plays. To us, a Broadway success meant a good show, a play you wanted, needed to see."

Partly because the Broadway shows drew such poor attendance and partly because not even the herculean McKennon could endure the rigors of three-night stands, three more plays were added to the repertoire, making a six-night run possible. The "new" plays were old tent show favorites: *The Old Grouch, Peg o' My Heart* and *Laff That Off*. By mid-season the three Broadway plays were replaced by three more tent show plays. Uniformed usherettes, reserved tickets, and other trappings of the "professional" theatre were also discarded.

The company trouped discouragingly through the rural South, then discovered somewhat larger audiences once they had crossed the Red River into Texas; but operations remained discouragingly unprofitable. After seventeen weeks, the McKennon Players closed their season in Odessa, Texas. Manager McKennon stated in a *Billboard* article that "business was consistently poor all season, not a performance grossing the nut [i.e. expenses]." The show equipment, including a 60 x 170 foot tent, four semi-trailers with tractors, 1,600 chairs and a large electric generator were trouped to Los Angeles, to be stored in the elephant barn of the old Lincoln Park Zoo. The McKennons settled at their nearby home for the winter, hoping to regroup for the following season.

Planning sessions were interrupted one day by a phone call from Harley Sadler, who was in session with the Texas Legislature. Would the McKennons be interested in joining forces for the coming season? Would they! Everyone knew of the almost legendary Harley Sadler and the magic that his name possessed at the box office. The prospect of their huge tent filled to overflowing with West Texas audiences delighted the McKennons.

In truth, the telephone call was not totally unexpected. Burnie Massengale, Harley's ever-faithful brother-in-law, had worked as a canvasman for the McKennons the previous season; the thought that he might be scouting the show for Harley had occurred to both Joe and Marian. The phone call confirmed their suspicions, and also indicated that Burnie had given Harley a favorable report.

The prospective partnership seemed almost an accomplished fact to the McKennons as they were met at the Austin airport by Sweetwater's State Representative. They could not help, however, but be a little apprehensive. "We were tense," Marian recalled in a recent interview, "—but you couldn't be tense with Harley. He was so relaxed, so cordial, so warm, that by the time we had finished dinner that evening there was no question that we'd known Harley for a very long time.... Billie was more reserved, beautifully turned out, very chic, very cordial, very smooth—but Harley was the main attraction."

An agreement was quickly worked out and within a few months the Sadler-McKennon show was on the road. Responsibilities were divided between the two managers. Joe was in charge of the equipment, of put-up and tear-down, and getting the company from one location to another. Harley ran the actors, the show, and handled the ticket sales, with Billie serving as business manager.

The arrangement worked in the following fashion. When the show arrived in a town, Harley would come down to the lot, usually a choice downtown location, one which the owner would rent only to Harley. The popular showman, his hair thinning and turning a little gray, remained only long enough to explain how the tent should be positioned, since he felt that placement of the marquee greatly affected the drawing power of the show, a position he had maintained throughout his years of setting-up. Having discussed this matter with his new partner, Harley would leave before crews began rolling out the canvas. Joe McKennon, from lifelong habit and firm conviction, knew that canvas never hung properly unless it was cursed into a suitable state of limpness. Harley had never allowed any profanity on his show, but with Joe an equal partner, about all he could do under the circumstances was leave before the air turned blue. "It made Harley unhappy to hear Joe swear," Marian McKennon said, "and we all tried not to make Harley unhappy."

At show time, Sadler and his company would take over the tent, while McKennon and his workers lounged around on the lot. The arrangement proved to be a workable division of authority, with each boss trying not to intrude upon the territory of the other. The division of authority proved workable—which is not to say that some friction did not develop.

Although the prohibition against profanity was bent to accommodate McKennon, Harley's no-drinking rule remained, since it was favored by both the partners. Joe, after conquering his youthful problems with alcohol, had become a dedicated abstainer. Harley, even though he had taught himself to drink socially, desperately wanted a sober company for his farewell tour. An employment ad which he placed in *Billboard* stated in bold capitals:

"IF YOU DRINK (EVEN OCCASIONALLY) DON'T ANSWER."

Undoubtedly Harley viewed this return to the road as a means of partially rehabilitating his wife. Billie had not responded well to being a housewife. Harley had withdrawn from show business not too long after Gloria had been taken from her. With a husband gone much of the time on business or political matters, she found herself continually at loose ends. Alcohol helped to fill the void of a life that had suddenly become empty, meaningless.

To shield his wife from temptation, Harley became uncharacteristically harsh and unforgiving. In spite of his rigid job specification, there was one drinking actor on the show, a talented performer whose wife—with sympathetic help from Joe McKennon—contrived to keep him out of Harley's path when he was not in sober condition. But one blazing hot Texas morning, the intoxicated actor stumbled onto the lot, singing a ditty which scorched the ear of passing townspeople. McKennon corraled him, dosed him liberally with black coffee, and barricaded him in the cab of one of the trucks, pending the onset of sobriety.

Sitting in this truck, hubcap deep in a field of weeds, the pie-eyed performer gave what McKennon describes as one of the greatest pantomime performances he has ever witnessed. Grasping the wheel, the actor threaded his way through heavy city traffic, honked the horn and shook his fist at little-old-lady drivers, gunned his motor in defiance of a passing policeman, clashed gears as he fought his way up a steep grade, clutched the wheel in terror as his brakes failed on a sharp curve, and died in flaming agony as the truck ran over a cliff. But each time he died, he recovered to drive again. Such a happy-drunk story deserves a happy ending, but it was not to be. Harley came to the lot while the actor was still in his cups and fired him on the spot.

The show was a box office success, with crowds coming out in record numbers. A single "all time, anywhere" record for a single tent show performance was set in Post, and an all time record for weekly attendance was set in Lubbock shortly afterwards, with 18,000 attending during the six day run. Civic groups vied with one another in honoring their friend. Gifts of Indian blankets, cowboy hats, boots, traveling cases were presented with appropriate ceremony and genuine affection. Perhaps the most impressive gift came from a group of well-wishers who invaded the stage in Lubbock during Harley's curtain speech. He was presented with a diamond-studded wristwatch, on the back of which was engraved

To Harley

From Lubbock.

Farewell tours, whether that of Sarah Bernhardt or Judy Garland or Harley Sadler, have a certain sadness about them. The faithful followers, grayer, paunchier, are still there in record numbers, but their children are not, having found entertainment elsewhere. The idol of the hour is a ghost of what he was, offering an imitation of what he once had been. For the true believers, the imitation is good enough, but the discerning can tell the difference. Rolland Haverstock, who had grown up watching both his father and Harley play the red-haired Toby roles, viewed these performances with sadness. "The heart had gone out of it," he said.

Still, the fifty-five year old performer appeared in the same silly-kid roles that he had played more than thirty years before, but now makeup was applied heavily in an effort to conceal the lines of age. He had difficulty concentrating on the show. Oilmen were constantly flying in and out, needing to consult the showman about one or another of his wells. Politicians, well aware of Harley's vote-getting capabilities, swarmed like flies around a sugar bowl. Harley was as usual, always available. One night the curtain was over a half-hour late going up because the showman-senator and some of his performers were appearing at a Democratic rally in Lubbock's MacKenzie Park.

The tour was difficult for a frail man who was beginning to show symptoms of a heart condition. As if the show were not enough to consume his energies, money worries kept him continually on the move among his various oil leases. Leaving the tent shortly after the evening's performance, he would drive to wherever his rig was punching a hole in the dry West Texas crust, spending the day in discussion and decision making. Catching a few hour's sleep, often in the rear seat of his car, he would drive back to the show, arriving in time to greet another tent full of well-wishers. In other times Harley had usually gone to his trailer when he left the stage, spending free moments visiting with friends. Now a chair for him was placed in the wings, and he collapsed into it as soon as he came offstage. No one spoke to him as he sat there, gathering his strength for the next entrance.

He was also burdened by problems resulting from the partnership. With two such divergent personalities in charge, members of the company polarized, becoming either one of McKennon's people or one of Sadler's. Salaries were a sore point; loyal old-timers were willing to work for Harley for less than Joe had to pay apprentice canvasmen with no experience. There was a dispute between the partners over division of the bally candy proceeds. One of Sadler's people was suspected of skimming the receipts from reserved seat sales.

Billie continued to drink, and in her muzzy-headed condition, she confused plusses and minuses in her records, causing further tension between the partners. Drinking, she was quarrelsome, tending to view the world with an alcoholic paranoia. Harley had difficulty controlling her at times.

The show closed in November, with the traditional banquet in San Angelo. The tour was a raging success from an audience standpoint, but whether either partner made much money is doubtful. The McKennons bought a house in Abilene, and after putting the show in winter quarters eight miles from town, set about making plans for the ensuing season.

Harley and Billie returned to Sweetwater, to find that the entire town had turned out to fete their favorite son with a "Flowers for the Living" celebration. Bouquets, floral and verbal, were presented to Harley while he was still around to appreciate them. There was a chuckwagon dinner, testimonials, gifts and an address by Governor Buford Jester, who expressed his pleasure that he would not have to face Sadler as a rival in the coming election.

The next year, the Sadlers moved to Abilene, buying a house not far from the McKennon's residence. Harley leased his name as "presenter," so that Joe's troupe could go out as

HARLEY SADLER PRESENTS

THE MARIAN MCKENNON PLAYERS

For use of his name, Harley was to receive 25% of the gross income, with the understanding that he would direct the shows for the company and make occasional guest appearances. However, pressures of business and politics kept the showman away from the show for the entire summer, causing considerable discontent. The McKennons felt that Harley had reneged on his verbal commitment to direct and make appearances; the audiences who came expecting to see their old favorite felt cheated when they found he was not with the show.

The following year, after a disastrous fire in Littlefield

which destroyed the large tent, the McKennons took out a smaller show featuring a bill of straight Toby plays— without the Sadler name. Audience response did not justify another season. In later years, Joe McKennon became a gentleman farmer in North Carolina, curator and consultant for the Ringling Circus Museum, wheelwright for ailing circus wagons, author of the first history of the carnival and a century-spanning saga of the circus. He also became a specialist in presenting elaborate fireworks displays for large celebrations.

Except for a few benefit performances of *Saintly Hypocrites and Honest Sinners* with an amateur company, the McKennon-Sadler tour marked the end of Harley's stage career. Other cares, other responsibilities came to the front, and there was little time left for show business. Besides, tent theatre was no longer the money-making proposition it had once been; Harley could not afford such an unprofitable indulgence.

Chapter Eleven

Last Act

IN 1950 HARLEY was flat broke, wiped out by a succession of dry holes. Wildcatting is a high risk business, a little like pitching pebbles into a pond hoping to find one that will float. Occasionally, almost miraculously, a floater turns up, making amends for the mountain of pebbles resting on the bottom. Sadler had been waiting for some time for the miracle stone to appear.

Poverty did little to change his life style since his credit remained solid. Based on past performance, everyone confidently believed that Harley would contrive to pay his debts—eventually. Having no money did not stop him from picking up the check for every luncheon or dinner party, but now he signed the bills rather than paying them. His restaurant tabs in Austin and Abilene grew ever longer.

In 1952 a mild heart seizure put him in the hospital. Though not severe, it should have been a stern warning to a sixty-year-old whose father and two older brothers had all succumbed to heart attacks. At an age when he should be thinking of retirement, this politician-showman-wildcatter remained everybody's man, dashing from the Panhandle to the Permian Basin to the Rio Grande Valley in response to requests to speak at a political rally, conduct a charity auction, emcee a benefit. Obviously he was asking more of his frail body than it could provide. "The ham in me put me in the hospital," he said to a reporter, grinning up at him from his sick bed. "It's just vanity, I guess, wanting to do everything people ask me to do." He resolved to refuse at least a few of the many invitations, but he never kept that resolve.

Sensing that his time was limited, the out-of-luck oilman drove himself to the limit in his efforts to achieve some financial security. Billie's drinking problem had progressed to full-fledged alcoholic addiction, and providing for her weighed heavily on his mind. Evenings, Billie worked as manager of a drive-in but she had little to do with her days,

Talent Show

Featuring
Harley Sadler
As Master of Ceremonies

Tues. Oct. 12
7:30 P.M.

Avoca
High School

Sponsored by P-TA

Benefit of Local Boy
Scouts and Cub Scouts

Talent from Surrounding Towns Participating.
Prizes Awarded

Admission — 25 & 50c

Contestants Contact
A. C. JENSEN, R. T. TAYLOR
Or CLYDE WORKMAN, Committee

Harley's last stage appearance.

since her husband left the house around daybreak and seldom returned until late in the day. Each morning, before he departed, Harley would routinely search the cabinets and closets for hidden bottles, pouring what he discovered down the kitchen sink. But no sooner had he left than a cab driver (the standard bootlegger of the Bible Belt) would arrive, bringing a fresh supply.

Although the "Ledge" paid pitifully little and public service was a luxury he could ill afford, Sadler could not bring himself to say "no" when filing time for re-election came around in 1954. He won nomination without opposition.

Having taken an interest in prisons and rehabilitation, he felt that he could not refuse an invitation to appear at the Huntsville Prison Rodeo, an annual event which drew large crowds from all over the state. While there, he contracted pneumonia, not severe in itself, but certainly sufficient reason to take it easy for a while. Still recuperating, he received a request for help at a Boy Scout fund-raising affair in Avoca, one of his many home towns. How could he refuse?

Joel Grimes, pastor of Avoca's First Baptist Church, was among the first to greet the showman when he arrived at the school auditorium. "Harley, you're not looking at all well," Brother Joel said, concern written on his face.

"I know it," Harley replied. "Doctor told me the red light was on." He sighed, but then the famous lop-sided grin spread across his face. "You know, Joel, if the Good Lord saw fit to call me tonight, I don't know of any place I'd rather be than right here, among old acquaintances and loved ones."

Within an hour, he was stricken onstage. Rushed to a nearby hospital in Stamford, he died twelve hours later, on October 14, 1954. Billie and his brother, Ferd, were at his side.

The funeral was massive and impressive. The Governor, Senators, state and national political figures, millionaire oilmen, actors and countless ordinary people came to pay their last respects. Norman Bonds, Harley's semi-adopted son, had the task of receiving dignitaries arriving at the Abilene airport. He recalls that all of them said the same thing as they took his hand in sympathy: "Harley was my best friend." Bonds also remembers an overall-clad workman who lingered long at the casket, then uttered the same words as the mighty: "He was my best friend."

Sadler's will made a few specific bequests, such as leaving the diamond-studded watch given him by the people of Lubbock to the Museum of Texas Technological College, but the bulk was left to his widow. No one is inclined to overvalue the worth of an estate, inheritance taxes being what they are; even granting a considerable understatement, the near-poverty of Sadler's condition was startling. Including house, personal belongings, oil properties, leases and automobile, the total worldy goods of this man who made a million dollars from a tent show was valued at a little over six thousand dollars. "He gave himself away," said Maurice Brookes, the attorney and close friend who probated the will. "If he didn't have any money in his pocket, he'd borrow from me or somebody else and give it away to whoever asked him for help."

Billie was appointed executrix, under the terms of the will. By selling off most of the oil holdings, she was able to pay the major outstanding debts, even the unrecorded ones which surfaced after Harley's death. She found work as cashier in an Abilene drug store, and her paycheck, combined with occasional royalty payments from oil rights, provided a living. She had to care for her brother Burnie, who was no longer able to work because of increasing debility caused by mustard gas inhaled during the First World War.

Mary Roberts, an old friend of Gloria's, recalls handing money across a counter to the clerk and realizing with a start that the clerk was Gloria's mother.

It was such a shock to me to see Billie Sadler in this unglamorous role after the years of gazing up at her position on the pedestal I had constructed for her in my mind.

She was still exquisitely groomed and gracious, but the grief and torture she was drowning in were very evident in her eyes. Our exchange of greetings was very brief and strained. I think we both wished it hadn't happened.

Marjorie Hager, one of Gloria's closest friends, urged Billie to move down in the Valley with her, to the little town of Donna. Billie replied,

I did so appreciate you asking me to come and stay with you all. But Marjorie I guess my life in a way is laid out for me, as long as Burnett lives. He has been very ill with flu and I've had him in the hospital. Brought him home yesterday. I went back to work at the drugstore on the 2nd of November as I felt that in a way it was best for me. I work from 2 p.m. until 10 p.m.—which helps take care of the evenings, I guess, but for the last week had to take a leave of absence on acct. of his illness. I am still living in the G[illegible] apt. which I guess is just as well, as nothing matters anymore.

I am trying so hard Marjorie but I feel the breaking point is just around the corner. Harley always said, Billie, you can take it, but he was here then, even tho the road was rough I could lean on him and he on me. But now the days seem to be alright, but the nights are so lonely, usually he would be home from work, listening to the radio and reading the paper. In his little old sweet way, he would say, well [how?] are you, and then, darling I know you are tired. And so many times he would have some kind of a little lunch fixed. Marjorie I just can't explain to the outside world. I try to carry on but within and when I am alone my heart is breaking. God and God alone can give me solace and comfort for which I pray every minute.

There was worse to come for Harley's widow. A few months after his death, Billie developed a lump under her tongue which would not go away. A trip to the M.D. Anderson Cancer Clinic, in Houston, confirmed her worst fears. A disfiguring operation followed: her speech became slurred and she drooled constantly, had difficulty keeping her tongue in her mouth. She moved, with Burnie, to an Austin apartment, and refused to see any of the old friends who called. No amount of trouble or sorrow had ever prevented Billie from facing the world; but for this once-beautiful woman, being disfigured was more than she could bear.

One person she did see was Roy Payne, an Abilene oil friend of Harley's who now had a position with the Texas Railroad Commission. Would he serve as Burnie's legal guardian after she was gone? Payne agreed to serve without pay as trustee for Billie's dwindling estate, hoping to be able to provide $150 a month required to care for her brother.

Shortly after the will was signed, Payne had a frantic phone call from Burnie: Billie had gone to bed and wouldn't wake up. Fast work by a hospital crew saved her from death by overdose. Ferd Sadler hurried to her bedside from his home in Dexter, New Mexico. "Billie," he said solicitously, "I don't want you to do anything like that again."

She turned her face toward the bare hospital wall. "Don't worry," Billie replied grimly, "Next time I'll do a better job."

Ferd and his wife, Gladys, were Billie's tie with the Sadler family. Shortly after being discharged from the hospital, Billie, with her brother, drove to Dexter, where Ferd was postmaster. It was a short, sad visit; Billie was obviously dying. "It's gone down into my lungs," she confided to her brother-in-law. "I'm having trouble breathing."

She chose to forego a lingering, agonizing death. On July 29, 1955, ten months after Harley's death, she went into her bedroom, closed the door, and shot herself.

By careful husbanding of what money and oil rights remained in the estate, Roy Payne was able to provide for the ailing Burnie for the ten years that he was to live. Room and board were arranged at the Wooten Hotel, in Sweetwater, where Don Wooten, an old friend of Harley's was manager. Because Burnie was not able to handle money, Payne had to pay all his bills for these ten years and provide small but regular amounts of spending money. "Burnie was not," his trustee says, "any great trouble."

Bob Huff, a Lubbock attorney and close friend of the Sadlers, provides a note on the final closing of the Sadler books. When Harley died, Huff received a check for $2,500 in payment of an interest-free loan he had made his old friend some time before. No sooner had he opened the envelope containing the check than he had a call from Billie. Money was tight at the moment, and would he mind holding the check for a while? Huff not only didn't mind but he tore up the check and forgot about it. At Billie's death, he received a check for the full amount from Roy Payne with a note explaining that it came from Billie's insurance money and that she had been concerned that this debt be erased. Thus, the Sadlers passed from the scene with the slate wiped clean, owing nothing to anyone.

The city cemetery in Cameron, where the three Sadlers share the Massengale family plot, nestles among the rolling hills of Central Texas. An older section, shaded by massive live oaks, contains ancestors whose limestone markers have been all but obliterated by the passing seasons. There is a newer addition, sun-baked and flat, where the blockish granite markers sit upon the still-raw earth of the new graves. The Massengales and Sadlers lie on the edge of the oldest part of the graveyard. A small but ornate marker, limestone enclosing a marble urn, looks as though it was originally intended for Gloria and her husband. Instead, the joint headstone marks the resting places of father and daughter. Billie, the last to go, lies below them, her grave marked by a small granite slab.

The surroundings are pleasant, with that air of peacefulness so often found in small town burying grounds. Whoever used to send the sexton an annual fifteen dollars to care for the Sadlers and Massengales has apparently passed on, and a tough bermuda grass is beginning to clutch at the base of the markers. As the years pass, the slightly acidic rain dripping from the live oaks will erase the names from the limestone, wiping clean the only monument that was ever raised to this West Texas showman.

Index

Compiled by Samuel Stark